Do It Yourself Publishing

Do It Yourself Publishing

✦

How To Have Fun And Make Money In Independent Publishing

*An Updated Version of How to Write a Best-Seller
While Keeping Your Day Job!
A Step-by Step Manual of Success for Writers Who
Want to Be Published But Don't Have the Time.
Do it Now!*

Daniel H. Jones

iUniverse, Inc.
New York Lincoln Shanghai

Do It Yourself Publishing
How To Have Fun And Make Money In Independent Publishing

iUniverse, Inc.

For information address:
iUniverse, Inc.
2021 Pine Lake Road, Suite 100
Lincoln, NE 68512
www.iuniverse.com

ISBN: 0-595-30847-3

Printed in the United States of America

Thanks to the good Lord for all my blessings and challenges.

Contents

Acknowledgments

Of course, this effort wouldn't have happened without the love and patience of my wife and kids-thanks for making it all worthwhile! Thanks to all the good folks at River Oaks Books in Houston for their continued support of my mother, Jeanne and my brother Michael at the store. Thanks to my brother Casey for Butterfly Lane.

Special thanks to my Dad for his continued support.

1

I suppose the old maxim that one can't serve two masters is true. I'm now unemployed. Rather, than bore you with details let's just stay positive and pro-active and move on with the business of this effort which began as a new and improved version of *How to Write a Best-Seller While Keeping Your Day Job!* but has evolved into something wider in scope. I was last unemployed in 1997. Although that was a trying time, many blessings came to me including but not limited to, spending quality time with my young children and the creation of my successful debut-novel *St. Jude's Secret*. I *know* there's an even greater blessing in the works this time. I've placed my trust and faith in my Creator and as long as I surrender my worries to Him, stay positive and keep growing spiritually things will work out. One way of looking at it is that I seem to be finally following my bliss as Joseph Campbell would say. I like this business of writing and publishing independently. It's been a great adventure. Funny thing too, once you really commit to something you really want to do, the Universe miraculously comes to your assistance. I think Goethe said that, but don't quote me on that please. I have seen it happen in my life but more often than not I have blocked that assistance. But no more!

Let's open up to the universal assistance right now and go for it. Granted, there have been changes, set-backs and growth spurts in the publishing industry since I published *How to Write a Best-Seller While Keeping Your Day Job!* However, there's never been a better time to publish independently. Please read on to learn why I say that and then do it yourself.

As with my previous effort, this little book is offered as an outline of possible steps in the journey to publication. Again it's born of the usual writer's angst at staring for far too long at a blank page, re-directed nervous energy and a burgeoning notion that it may actually be helpful to somebody. This notion dawned on me after an interview with my local newspaper on my novel's journey to publication in a feature with several other local independents. The feature was about publishing independently and the then new print-on-demand technology. The interview got exposure for my novel, but the focus was the process. "How are you doing this?" was really the subject of the interview. That was the key.

Additionally, I discussed the process with several friends, neighbors and co-workers who were genuinely interested in exploring their publishing options without re-inventing the wheel, as I have. Moreover, my mother and older brother often serve as listening-posts at their bookstore. They support independents and often provide a sounding board for local writers with manuscripts and book ideas. Mom and older brother have not hesitated to share my contact information with some very kind and talented people. I am very grateful for that and hope I've helped a few folks. I hope this effort helps even more.

So, here we go. This piece is meant to be an easy, quick-reference guide outline, handbook, whatever you choose to call it. Its aim is to assist you in creating, publishing and marketing commercially viable books. Something that you, as a writer can arm yourself with as you enter the book business battleground. Consequently, please note that each chapter will be formatted as a **10 Point Attack** Plan. But first, let me begin by doing a little housekeeping:

1. I will not get bogged down in technical things. You can find how-to books on everything from proper manuscript form to proper manuscript submission on your own. Besides, that's no fun! It's not fun for me to write (remember that nervous energy) and not fun and easy for you to follow. Just to let you know, I have a favorite Rolling Stones CD *the* classic live "Get Yer Ya-Ya's Out" blaring and NFL Football on the tube. The wife and kids are out of the house for a few hours and I've just popped the top on a cool one. This *is* fun and it can be profitable. The traditional retail book business is a cranky old beast. Best to let it be. Keep your enterprise fun and positive and it will be profitable.

2. Here's the caveat emptor. If you haven't got the picture yet, this manual <u>does not</u> offer a sure-fire method to get published by a <u>traditional</u> publisher. Although I have enjoyed success and have been assisted and guided by many good people, my own journey to publication was fraught with more than the usual up's and down's of getting fiction published including but not limited to disingenuous literary agents, publishers and promotional folks. In fact, it was the "back-burnering" (devastating to me at the time, but a common practice in the industry whereby a publisher doesn't publish one's accepted manuscript and keeps the rights!) of *St. Jude's Secret* by a publisher in 1999 that led to my publishing with the print-on-demand publisher, <u>www.iUniverse.com</u>. Print-on-demand is now a not-so-new technology in publishing that allows out-of-print books to be re-printed and works of previously published and unpublished authors' works to be

electronically created and digitally stored then printed in a traditional book format once an order for the book is received. There is a nominal upfront fee for this service. My experience has been with www.iUniverse.com but there are other print-on-demand publishers such as www.1stbooks.com and X-libris. Additionally, you now see individuals setting up genre-specific websites and affiliating with the POD publishers.

3. POD publishers aren't vanity publishers. You've seen the ads. Manuscripts wanted. Let me tell you something. Unless you have your own sure-fire distribution system, those books are going nowhere. Then you're stuck with two-thousand copies of your 75,000 word manuscript (two-hundred and fifty page book) that likely cost you upwards of $10,000 to produce through the vanity/subsidy press. The books will sit in your garage or storage area. Need a bunch of doorstops? Then go with a vanity press. POD books are different. A POD book now can cost as little as $7 per copy to produce regardless of the number of copies ordered and printed and there's no distribution nightmare for you or the POD publisher. Essentially, POD publishers provide the enterprising and entrepreneurial writer an efficient and quality, turn-key vehicle to get his or her work to the marketplace. However, please be aware of the limitations and keep reasonable expectations. Just as in traditional publishing, POD success doesn't come overnight or without growing pains. But, the adventure is worth it. Now, with e-books and e-classes gaining popularity the sky's the limit!

2

Life has a way of getting in the way of the Great American Novel, doesn't it? All for the good, though. I mean writing can't really occur without living can it? No. Not really. And with the typical advance for a first time novelist averaging in the $1,500.00-2,500.00 range, life and its gainful employment prerequisite better get in the way! With POD, your day job can support the writing habit. The odds of getting an agent and a deal for a non-fiction book proposal are better but I don't see where the advances are greater. See, the book business is so bottom-line now that unless you are a big name like Grisham or a recent newsmaker, you're not going to get a contract from a traditional publisher. Even if you do, the marketing is still going to be up to you and on your nickel.

So let's start this journey off with marketing and promotion. That's because it's probably the biggest and least prepared for hurdle the grass-roots writer will encounter. So, let's begin with the assumption you have completed your compelling, commercially viable work and have gone through the submission process with your POD publisher of choice. So how do you get folks to buy it? Remember, we're assuming a modest budget here, too. One your spouse or life-partner will let you get away with!

Promotion. 10 point attack Plan

1. Set up a business for expenses. A sole proprietorship is the easiest, cheapest and most effective tool for tax purposes. Choose a DBA and pay the nominal filing fee in your area. Save all promotional expense receipts for tax time! Besides, this is your writing and publishing business.

2. UPDATE! Make flyers and business cards. This is still the cheapest and probably the most bang-for-your-buck weapon in your promotional arsenal. Try to come up with an angle or catchy slogan. For example, my novel *St. Jude's Secret* features the hot topic of genetically modified foods and in particular coffee. So, I went to a very reasonable business card store around the corner from my office and about 24 hours I had cards to leave all over town. The cards asked "Is your Coffee safe?" and featured my title and where to get it. Same thing with flyers. Do them up on your computer, print them out and pin them up at local college bulletin boards or message kiosks around town. Leave them at coffee shops or ask merchants to feature them. The POD publishers have now gotten in on this and are charging for it. Unfortunately, all the better-known POD publishers have increased their entry-level package prices ($459.00 at iUniverse and $598.00 at 1stbooks). However, they now offer a basic marketing toolkit of promotional items including templates for sell-sheets, bookmarks, flyers and press-kits. From what I've seen it's worth the price. They're using the digital technology now to produce quality promotional items that are slick and do not have the home-made look that can get you thrown right into the dumpster. So, gone are the days of the $99.00 plan at iUniverse, but the prices are still reasonable when you consider the nicely done promotional stuff. But you may not want to throw out your Elmer's Glue and two-brad, pocket folders just yet. And keep your business cards.

3. UPDATE! Plan your Promotional efforts in a timely manner. This sounds simple but it's not. Typically, there was a gap of about 6 weeks from the date your POD book goes "live" to the date that it's readily available through normal retail channels. That has been *cut in half* that time now as POD publishers have gotten their act together. As the author, you'll receive several free copies before your book goes live. Moreover, you can order the book for yourself about a week or two after going live. (More on this in POD submission section). You won't get traditional galleys with a POD book. Be prepared to order a minimum of 25 books yourself, from the POD publisher as soon as you are able to do so. You'll see why in a moment. It all dovetails. You've got to be ready when this happens!

4. UPDATE! Get your Press Kit together. Now, you can have your own or order something more professional-looking from the POD publisher so you can compete with traditionally published books. I keep using that term, but you'd be surprised to learn that quite a few small publishers use POD technology but have their traditional distribution network so the title gets into bookstores in the usual manner. Some small traditional publishers now have the POD book machine and produce POD books under their own block of ISBN's (distribution numbers on back cover). But as for press kits you can still do it the old-fashioned way as described before but use the POD publisher promo-material that you paid for and down-loaded. You may want to get a good picture of yourself to put in the press kit. I didn't do that until it was too late in the game. It could help to make for a professional presentation. Be sure to insert the synopsis you've generated for your book. Print the back cover write-up you'll have written for your book (more on this in POD submission chapter), print the press release you've generated in the POD publisher's format. This press release needs to be succinct, and if at all possible, it should have some connection to current events, local interests or some human interest element. Put copies of all the above along with a copy of your book in the folder. That's your press kit that you'll use to send to potential reviewers and interviewers. Be sure to think up 10 questions for an interviewer to ask you in connection with your book.

5. Contact and cultivate ties with local independent booksellers. This is still a biggie! Do it once your book goes live. Let them know it's coming. Give them a press kit. Visit and let them know what genre it's in for fiction or the subject matter for non-fiction. Get to know them if you don't already. Talk books. Buy books. Become a regular customer at your favorite local independent bookstore. Offer to *give* them promotional copies of your book as soon as you get one in your hot little hand. If it's good, they'll know. If it fits their clientele, they'll know that too. If they say they can't sell it in their store, don't get bent out of shape. That's their way of telling you what their customers tastes are. Move on to a store more suitable for your book. Locate stores in other towns and mail them a copy with your press kit. The key for you is to work patiently with a store in your area to develop someone who'll *hand sell* your book. Hopefully, you'll coordinate a signing with the store, but be prepared to get creative. Remember, it's *their* business so work with them. They may order your book directly from the publisher. Let them know the discount your POD publisher offers for direct orders for an author signing. Offer to take the returns off their hands or be prepared to purchase your book from the POD publisher and work an agreement for the retailer to sell your books on consignment. *Do* whatever it takes because a local bookseller, selling books the old fashioned way can still do more for your sales than an on-line retailer or chain bookstore. Remember, Grisham sold his first novel to independents and individuals right from the trunk of his car. Bring the store and its customers along on your journey to publication. Also, always have a copy with you when you travel. Then you can visit with and discuss your title with independents in other cities. On a trip to Seattle for my regular job a few years back, I gave one of my books to a well-known criminal defense attorney I spotted at the check-in gate then made my pitch to a wonderful independent in Seattle who told me they could sell my novel and would order it. You never know.

6. <u>UPDATED Get your book reviewed. Somewhere. Anywhere!</u> This is crucial. To do it, you'll need copies of your book to send to potential reviewers. So, as soon as you can order your book yourself from your POD publisher do it then send copies out for review. Yes, that takes money. But remember, in essence you have taken on the role of the publishing house. In other words, you are taking the risk. This is key to understanding the process. Don't go into it thinking *they* are going to do anything for you. You are them! I recommend starting with on-line review sources. You can search for them on any search engine, but I've found Ed's Internet Review to be a good starting place. Once your book is available at the various on—line retailers, then you need to e-mail on-line reviewers (this is a big deal at Amazon) yourself and see if they'd be interested in reviewing your book. They may buy it, but be prepared to offer a free copy to a reviewer in exchange for a review. Choose your reviewers wisely and always be courteous and remember they are helping you get to your readers. Turning to print reviewers, be advised that this is a tough nut to crack. I've had one newspaper book reviewer tell me that they can't review every book people want them to review. Understandable. That and the newness of the POD technology, have made it difficult for the grass roots author to get to the trough. But you must try anyway. So, send those promotional copies along with your press kit to the reviewers at your local paper and any others that come to mind. You can find the names and addresses in the paper or on-line or in *The Literary Marketplace*. Try the Midwest Review of Books, Kirkus Reviews and others. Your book may be the POD breakthrough.

7. <u>Get some ink! Any publicity is good publicity</u>. Send your press release to your local paper. I've found that the community sections of the paper are always looking for announcements. Tie your press release in with a community event or announcement such as Hometown High School graduate announces publication of his/her debut novel. Announce any signings in this manner too. I mentioned earlier that it's difficult to get a print review. You *can* turn this reality around to your advantage. I have found that your best bet to get ink in newspapers is to work the feature angle on the new technology that features your title book as a shining example. Be sure to announce your book's debut in any alumni magazines you receive, church bulletins or trade publications that are related to your business or businesses that are featured in your book. For example, a favorable review of my novel appeared in the *Journal of Maritime Commerce* due to my main character's involvement in Admiralty Law and the shipping business. I sent the reviewer a free copy of my book about six months ago. This is how you must build your writing publishing business! One final note on publicity. You may wish to hire a publicist. If you do, steer clear of those who want to charge you a large upfront retainer and then an hourly fee. They may discuss book tours and other events to market your book. It's a waste of money. First of all, your POD book <u>will not</u> even be on the shelves of these stores unless you bring them yourself. Secondly, nobody will be at these signings. So, get any ideas of being on some grand book tour out of your head. The big publishers only do that for the big names, or latest sensational tell-all type books, not for your great novel. Better to choose a publicist that you can pay as you go on a monthly basis or per specific request you may have. A publicist can get you booked on radio talk shows around the country, whereby you call in and discuss your book after the host has read it and your press kit. Generally, they'll ask you the interview questions you submitted in your press kit. www.Talion.com is a very helpful and reasonable publicist, specializing in book promotion. I've done many wonderful radio interviews booked by the folks at Talion. But keep you budget modest.

8. <u>Send copies to your local library and to large libraries</u>. Address lists and contacts are available on-line and well at the library! This is one area in which traditional publishers seem to have POD publishers out-gunned. They look for some institutional buying by libraries to get some monetary return on a 5,000 copy run for a debut novelist. Try to get some institutional buying for your book and wait for a break! It's coming if you keep the dream alive and keep the promotional wave moving.

9. <u>Book Clubs, Writing Groups, Writer's Conferences, Speaking Engagements</u>. Join as early and as often as you can. Of course, you're there to share and participate, but these groups and places provide you with an opportunity to talk with people one on one about your book. Who better than you to do it! There is some chance of institutional buying with national book clubs, but I've found it's best to just work with them on an individual basis. Word of mouth is better. So, if you know you're sister in Ohio is in a book club, send her one of your books and maybe she'll present it as a club read!

10. <u>UPDATE! The Internet and e-mail</u>. Set-up your own website. Do it however you can with your budget in mind, of course. This a great tool for book promotion. Of course, your POD publisher will feature your title for sale at their website. **www.iuniverse.com** allows authors to publish articles about their books on their website. Be sure you do this because these articles are generally pick-ed up by the big Internet search engines. Once your title is available at Amazon, you can e-mail anyone you like, information about and the link to your title on Amazon. I don't think the other on-line retailers have this feature. B&N.com has a link to **www.iUniverse.com**, but is otherwise limited in its marketing capabilities. **www.Amazon.com**, also allows you to promote your title right alongside big name authors in your genre. This was done by buying points through a sponsored results account but that's been discontinued. You may now recommend your title alongside others. Also, through Amazon's advantage program you can even provide the books yourself should you wish to have signed-copies for sale over the Internet. Additionally, Amazon allows customer reviews of your book. This is very helpful and can help to increase on-line sales of your title as more folks give their two-cents worth. But don't be fooled by the sales numbers. Your Amazon sales ranking may go from last place (say 2,000,000th place) to the top 50,000 in ranking overnight, but that may mean you've sold only 20 books. But 20 books is nothing to sneeze at in this business so stick with it! Of course, you'll want to e-mail any and all friends, family, work colleagues, school mates, old flames, anybody you think may have even the slightest interest in your book.

Finally, on-line reading groups and chat rooms can be a big help. Join the club or chat and participate with courtesy and genuine interest, then ask the members if you may share information about your book. I have made many on-line friends who have been kind enough to review my book on-line. Their reviews helped to create an on-line buzz in connection with *St. Jude's Secret*, which led to increased sales. I have been invited to be a guest author during club chats. Although on-line reading club members don't generally request free copies of your book, be prepared to do so. The good will can only help you over the long term. Now, I think I could do an entire section on the following sentences in the previous book.

Moreover, you should obtain and/or compile e-mail address lists and e-mail a compelling sales pitch out with an offer of freebies (your book in e-format) to those who'll go to Amazon.com and buy the hard-copy. This can really take off with some pre-planning!

I've got to expand on these two sentences for you. I know of at least one author who has hit Amazon's number one (Joe Vitale did it with his *Spiritual Marketing* and visit Joe at www.mrfire.com) using this promotional method and several others who have come close. The recognition that comes with hitting number one at Amazon of course means increased sales and can get you noticed and picked up by the publishing elite. Of course, their game plan nowadays is to pick you up based on your marketing success only to see if you can market to another level of success for them! Without a lot of promotional support from them, I might add. But be that as it may here's how the Amazon number one drive can work. I'll show you by way of example. Remember, this all depends on having access to a good and targeted e-mail list. No spamming allowed. I will put the complete e-mail copy in the glossary of this book but here's how it's done. You must network with other authors on-line and request copies of e-book versions of their work. Explain politely what you're doing and more than likely they will be glad to help because they figure it's more exposure for them. Then put your e-mail together and include those e-books as freebies for downloading if the targeted audience will buy your book at Amazon. Plan for the right time to get your email out and watch the momentum build as the title climbs the charts. I have yet to see this happen for fiction. I have not made it to number one myself, but *St. Jude's Secret* did crack into the top 10,000 best sellers (not bad for an unknown author with a debut, POD novel) through my Internet efforts. Maybe I'll get to number one with this little book! Or it could be you! Again see the glossary for an example of Amazon number one promotional correspondence.

3

Before I present the POD **10 Point Action Plan,** remember that your book is independently published. Always give people the name of your publisher but do not say self-published. Despite historical evidence to the contrary, there is a perception in our society attached to a self-published author akin to that associated with an honorable mention award winning contestant. Good try but you're still a loser! You can't change that perception, so don't waste your time trying. Just remember your POD book is not self-published or the product of a vanity press. You're independent and so is your book.

In a real sense, print-on-demand offers you a chance to exercise your freedom of speech and whether it's good speech or bad speech, will be determined in the marketplace of ideas once your book is available.

Several years ago, this effort I'm doing right now would have remained just a brief daydream that tempted me during some monotonous meeting or after a dull day of paper-pushing. If I did carry the idea through to a non-fiction book proposal, the bottom-line publishing elite would likely deep-six it. Or say you've written a compelling piece of fiction that so skillfully crafts conflict, description, character development, and plot so as to take one's breath away. You are the voice of the fly-over people. The flame that burns brightest. Mark Twain reincarnated. Dickens reborn! But there's one problem. You haven't been published before and you don't have a literary agent.

"Write a good book," the elite likes to say. "And you'll get published. We're always looking for that diamond in the rough." Not all of us have the time for them to find us. Moreover, the downsizing and merging that's gone on over recent decades has further diminished a first-timer's chance of leaping from a publisher's slush pile to the best seller list. Gone with the wind are the days of a genius like Maxwell Perkins taking a whole generation of writers under his wing. Some small publishers are trying to fill the gap, but it's a tough row to hoe. Forget about it! And get over it!

Print-on-demand offers you the chance to get your work out to the people who really matter, your readers! Let them decide for themselves on the merits and let your work earn its success. Hey-isn't that kind of the American Way? I think so.

10 Point Attack List. The Business of POD.

1. UPDATE Read and understand the Publishing Agreement. You can go to X-Libris.com or www.iUniverse.com and review each one's Publishing Agreement. Take the time to read and digest the publishing agreement. Print it out. Take the time to do that. It's fairly straightforward and you want see any wording tying up your rights for fifty years after you die! I suggest you highlight the dates for license termination, cancellation. Note that the royalty for printed units is 20% net to the publisher at www.iUniverse.com. Royalties are paid to the author for each quarter's sales at iUniverse with checks mailed within sixty days of quarter's end (I have never had a problem with royalty payments). NB: no royalty payment is made for direct sales to the author. The author keeps all other rights inclusive of film and subsidiary rights. iUniverse sets out what it calls its "non-exclusive contract" at www.iuniverse.com as one that "allows you to pursue arrangements with traditional publishers while enjoying a generous 20% royalty—higher than industry standards."

2. UPDATE! Discounts. To the author and to retailers. This is still a very important area. It's crucial to your whole effort that you understand that both chain and independent booksellers expect and operate with a discount system. Typically, the chains demand a 40% discount. Independents vary but expect some discount. Independents are aware that the typical POD publisher offers only a 25% discount. www.iUniverse.com offers a 40% on units purchased directly from them when the purchase is for an author signing. Now, with iU's Premiere Program you may opt for retail discounts of 50% but you get only 10 % in royalties rather than their normal 20% royalty. This can help you get it onto more shelves but you trade off the royalty. Retailers don't often get a 50% discount so that's nice, however, I would take the normal royalty if I were you. This is because your book is not going to get into any bookstores unless you have arranged for it to be there through your discussions with the store management. Moreover, the retail bookseller is likely going to be more interested in returning the books that do not sell. POD publishers do not offer returns (see point # 3). So, just buy the books yourself and sell them at a 50% discount with no returns or offer to take any books that do not sell off the retailer's hands. Once you've developed a good relationship with an independent and set up a signing, go into Author Events and schedule the event prior to your independent calling in his or her order. Be advised that the retailer must pay for the books by credit card at iUniverse. There's no invoicing.

3. Returns. The retail book business is the only business I know of, whereby books may be returned to the publisher for a credit. POD doesn't play by these rules and retailers don't like that. It's a problem, but not insurmountable. Retailers know that POD books can be viable. But unless it's for a signing, the retailer may limit his or her order to 2-5 books. That's cool. Don't have expectations of huge numbers. You're just trying to get on the shelf so you will be read. But remind the store that a signing will get them a 40% and explain how you can help generate a good turn-out offer to send invitations, do a flyer to promote the event. You could also offer to sell them copies you've purchased yourself at 50% off and they get to keep the returns. That won't help you with your royalties but it will show that you're serious about the book business and can help you down the line.

4. Proof your manuscript. Nothing will kill your book quicker, undo all your hard work in promotion and just ruin your day than typos and errors in your original manuscript. Believe me, I know from my own experience with the first *St. Jude's Secret* file. *Mary hand a Bittle Bamb.* Remember?

5. Electronically or by mail. Submit your manuscript on any platform or by mail. It's that easy. Go to your POD publisher's website and follow the instructions. In the summer of 2000, the newness of the technology resulted in some glitches. Submission of my manuscript wasn't that easy and I had to re-submit several times. www.iuniverse.com has worked or maybe grown out of the glitches.

6. Have your back cover synopsis ready. As you click through the submission process, you'll be asked to provide information for the back cover. Include a brief synopsis in journalistic style and your biography. If you know someone, an author, editor, professor or radio/TV personality who has read and enjoyed your manuscript, ask for their comments and put that on the back cover. You'll also be able to upload a personal photo. You may want to invest in a headshot.

7. UPDATED Choose Your Publishing Plan. I will submit this effort under a special discount plan for current iU authors at www.iUniverse.com. With the Select Plan (reg. Price $459.00 but $259.00 with my discount) I'll get 5 free books, a four-color cover, an ISBN, e-book set up and all the distribution (Ingram and Baker & Taylor). I used the more expensive plan but I will not use it again. I think POD publishers set out to have some sort of editorial process, but they found it just wasn't feasible. The more expensive plans include this "editorial" process which is really just a rubber-stamp type of deal that may make the first-time author feel good to be "accepted" into the higher echelon plan. I cannot recommend the costlier plans. The less expensive plan provides everything I'll need for this book and will get me an iUniverse PSA (Publishing Service Associate). This person will walk you through the key events in your journey to publication and can help you with any problems that develop.

8. <u>Design Your Cover. Submit any Photographs.</u> You can choose your colors. You can give the design department an idea of what you want. Probably best to keep it straightforward, so the design folks can't go too far astray. You can send photos you want to use. I've found iUniverse's covers to be the best of the POD's and to fit in seamlessly on retail shelves with the big boys' titles.

9. <u>The Proof Form.</u> Okay. Imagine it's a weekend. Your spouse is sipping margaritas with the gals on a junket in the beautiful, colonial town of San Miguel de Allende, Mexico. Coincidentally, she was there again in 2003. The kids are all over the house and you are witnessing a miracle: the sudden appearance of your title's cover and book block filling your laptop's screen. You have a limited time to make a limited number (50) of corrections on the form and send it back. A day goes by before you've come down from the euphoric rush of seeing your manuscript in book form. The next morning passes before you get all the downloads done and learn how to operate the block proof and correction sheet. The kids are still kicking up their heels and the spouse is still seeing the sights in San Miguel. Your heart is racing, the hair on the back of your neck bristling as you stare at yet another, heretofore unseen typo. Get the picture? Make time for your final proof. Celebrate the moment you first see it with your best beloveds. Then let all your loved ones know that you need time, space and quiet to concentrate.

10. <u>Proof your manuscript.</u> Did I say this already? Nothing will kill your book quicker, undo all your hard work in promotion and just ruin your day than typos and errors in your original manuscript. Yes, run your spelling and Grammar Check, but have somebody else look it over. I don't care if you were an English major in college! Pay a copy editor, if necessary. Check your local listings or look on-line, search writers resources for a reasonable copy editor. Nothing will kill your book quicker, undo all your hard work in promotion and just ruin your day than typos and errors in your original manuscript. There. I said that again. Or was that an extra cut-and-paste? See what I mean? Re-do's of your manuscript can be done but there's a cost. Get it right the first time. If you can't make all the corrections in the limited space and time, it's decision time. Press on regardless or back up and punt? Start over and pay another submission fee? It's up to you. Best to get it right before you submit it the first time.

4

Enter the arena. Dare to fail! I saved the best for last. The writing process. The fun part! But just how does one write a compelling book? Moreover, what makes me think I can tell writers how to write a compelling piece of fiction? Why listen to me when they're are hundreds of books on the craft of writing available by folks with far greater credentials than I have? I'm not sure that I can. I know I can't share great insights into writing that haven't already been shared. I can tell you, however, I've made every mistake that growing writers make as they make their journey to publication. I've tried to learn from my mistakes and I've tried to keep the dream alive just as you have. I'm telling myself how to write as I convey some ideas on writing to you and recalling the thrust of this little red book, I want to keep it simple and in a format those pressed for time can easily digest and readily utilize. This list is by no means definitive but I think it can help the grass-roots author <u>compete</u> with the name authors and the big publishing mills. Hopefully, you find some fresh ideas. Here goes. Don't forget to have fun!

<u>10 point Attack Plan for a Compelling Novel.</u>

1. <u>Turn off the Internal Censor.</u> Do whatever you need to do to knock out that little voice inside your head that insists that you can't write anything worthwhile. I've found that this censor is in place to keep you from trying to write for fear of failing. Nothing new there, of course. Here are some ideas to help you get rid of the censor: Imagine you're writing on paper towels, napkins or tissue. Better yet go ahead and write on a paper napkin a scene, some dialogue, a setting. You will revise and transfer it later, but just the idea that the paper is disposable helps lower your internal censor's expectations and consequently, it's nervous, negative patter. Collage or storyboard your story. Cut and paste pictures, drawings, newspaper articles, and notes on a poster board or stick these items to a bulletin board above your desk. This will help your story write itself somewhat as you use the images you've cut and pasted to ignite your imagination. The censor can't argue with a story that's coming to life on its own. Take a notepad with you when you go out and let ideas come to you, rather than pressing too much while you're at your desk. Anything that let's you take yourself, your time constraints and your writing project less seriously can help turn off the internal censor and keep you writing through tough cases of writer's block.

2. <u>Write with your voice</u>. Trust who you are and that your unique world-view is worthwhile. Put your voice into every scene, every description, and every bit of dialogue. The voice of a piece of fiction is what makes it distinct form other works. A work with a strong voice will always carry more weight than a piece that is contrived to meet someone else's expectations. It's a hard thing to define and harder to catch it and hold onto it. I'll say this about an author's voice. It's that moment when you are able to step back and put that little twist on a phrase, sentence or paragraph that really sums things up for you as the writer. The voice is distinguishable as it manifests itself in characters but it's distinct and certain throughout a book. Agents, editors, writers and most importantly, readers know when a novel has a strong, genuine voice and it's often the most compelling component of a novel. Go with your voice. As your writing skills grow, you'll learn how to focus the voice and how to sometimes temper it, but trust it.

3. <u>Conflict</u>. You've got to have conflict in every scene of your book. Introduce it early and often. If your book is a murder mystery, open with the death and throw as many obstacles as you can think of in your main character's journey to solve the case. Introduce conflict into all dialogue, and relationships between characters as often as you can. By that I mean that if one character wants cream in her coffee, make sure her partner and/or adversary won't give her the cream. It can be that simple. Conflict keeps a reader from putting your book down and keeps them entertained by your story and your voice. Your boss is riding you at work. Your spouse wants you to get off the couch and paint your kids' rooms. The kid brought home a failing grade and the dog dumped on the rug. It's everyday life and we take it for granted. I think that's why it's so often missing in manuscripts. Once you've completed a scene, check it and re-check it for conflict.

4. <u>C.O.T.S</u>. Color, Odor taste and smell. I'm reminded of a quote credited to Walker Percy. It's said he instructed his students to "…describe the smell inside a Camelback-double on Magazine Street." For those of you not familiar with New Orleans, that's a shotgun house, usually in Victorian style, with a second floor about half-way back from the porch giving it it's distinctive camel's hump or back. Anyway, I think Mr. Percy wanted to get his students to draw the reader into that setting through his or her senses. It means so much more for the reader to make a mental association through the senses, so give the reader his money's worth. Of course the old adage "show-don't tell" fits right in here. Your characters should smell the red-pepper scented crab-boil until it brings a tear to your character's eyes. Let the faint hum of a streetcar disturb your character's telephone conversation and remind her of a tryst with a lover and so on. This leads right into the next point.

5. Weaving. Take the time to weave in C.O.T.S. as well as physical descriptions of people, places and things. Don't dump big chunks of description into scenes. You'll lose your reader! Subtly, weave the description into dialogue and action scenes. Take the time to weave as you go, but if mot, step back and do it during revision. Also, weave in bits of plot and punctuate with characters' reactions that show motivation. Again, show-don't tell. You can give your reader questions through plot weaving and you don't have to explain a whole lot to the reader. They really don't like it when a writer does that and they'll put the book down if you dump plot explanations or back story in a scene.

6. Scenes. I like to think of a novel as a long train of boxcars, rolling along. Each boxcar is a scene. The boxcar is carrying the scene's cargo (Characters, conflict, COTS, weaving, plot, dialogue. The train has a beginning. Middle and end. One box car hooks to the next. Each scene has to have a hook at the end to join it to the next. I've just run across a scene setting I shared with my son awhile back. It fits in here. Taking this a bit further, fill the boxcar with whatever your imagination comes up with and then go to the next boxcar and fill it and then connect them and you have the chapters of a book. It seems like a project too big to get a grip on, but if you take it a little at a time you'll have twenty 10-page boxcars before you know it.

7. Scene Outline. This is just an idea and may not work for you. I've drawn up a scene outline below:

Outline Chapter/Scene String 20-30 of these together and voila, you've got your novel!

I. The setting is:

    A. Time, place, environment:

        1. Details/brief description: Color, Odor, Taste Sight (COTS)

2. Memories from Character's Point of View:

3. Quotes and dialog:

A. Characters are:

　　1.Details brief description of characters:

　　2.Memories from Character:

　　3. Quotes & dialog:

B. Character Goals:

　　1.Details brief description of characters:

　　2.Memories from Character:

　　3 Quotes & dialog:

A. Scene Conflict always! ticking time-bomb

　　1. Main character vs. self, nature & other characters—

　　　　a. Details brief description of characters conflict

　　　　b.Memories from Character conflict

　　　　c. Quotes & dialog conflict

8. <u>Character POV</u>. Remember, once you are seeing the world from one character's Point of View, keep it that way. Sounds simple but it's easy to forget. Also, once you've opened up a character's POV, then you need to carry that character's story-line to the end of your novel and have resolution of that character's issues.

9. <u>Inner story/outer story</u>: The Inner story tracks the transformation your main character and other POV characters make as your outer story (action) progresses. Keep the inner story linked to the outer story. Do it subtly and weave it in as needed but don't go on for page after page. For instance your main character has a way with children and he kind of knows it but he can't give up the single life and settle down with his love interest. Offer the reader snippets that hint at the guy's love of children. The outer story is his journey with his love interest (with lots of conflict) toward settling down and raising a family. The more poignant or more genuine you can make those moments where inner transformational moments and outer story meet, the better. A good example is *Love is A Many Splendored Thing*. Jennifer Jones starts out as pretty tough cookie and a formidable catch for William Holden in the film. She's a widowed doctor in Hong Kong with a strong career, but right from the start, we see her caring for children and exalting warmth and commitment to family. She doesn't need William Holden, even if he is William Holden! But as she keeps reaching out to children and to her family in Chunking, her inner transformation takes place coincidentally with her outward courtship dance with Holden.

10. UPDATE! Hero's journey or arc.
This topic is often the subject of entire courses at writers' conferences and seminars. Most of you have this scheme pretty well pegged. Many of us grass-roots authors do not. That may not be all bad. There's certainly no room for a woman's way of handling things in this format. I mean women get together and talk about things and come up with alternative and successful ways of solving problems and resolving inner/outer story conflict. So, this Hero's Journey thing probably needs to be re-evaluated. Most of the fiction I read in high school and college was not all that well-mapped out and linear. So much of novel writing used to be for self-discovery and growth rather than following a pattern that would adapt well to the big screen. I mean people have made careers out of interpreting Faulkner and Joyce for the rest of us. I must say I have sensed a backlash within myself and in talking with some novelist friends to the whole idea of the Hero's Journey.

But it's out there. Although I cannot hope to grasp and convey its many complexities that renowned writing teachers and scholars have chronicled over the years, I'll give you my take on how it works. I can't recite to you all the players, roles and stages in the hero's journey. I'll stick with the basics as I understand them and trust you'll find this helpful.

Basically, there's not much new in storytelling, going back to Greek mythology. Some writing teachers say that if a writer strays too much from the tried and true methods which are based in myth and oral tradition, the reader will know it and drop your novel like Hercules dropped the Nemean Lion. I read *The Twelve Labors of Hercules* to my son a few years back over several nights. That's a good read for a primer on the hero's journey or story arc. In performing each labor, Hercules is **1.)** called to action (to bring Eurystheus the monster, man-eating lion's skin). Hercules is hesitant or reluctant but Jupiter's vindictive wife Juno makes Hercules obey Eurystheus. Then he **2.)** journeys to a special, faraway place to find his challenge. **3.)** He is confronted with problems which set him back when he faces the challenge (Nemean Lion survived his club and arrows). **4.)** He hits rock-bottom physically and mentally (bring in inner story issues) and **5.)** faces his certain death. **6.)** He re-groups learns something about himself (faith, strength) and his adversary that makes him stronger, tougher, smarter and assists him to **7.)** overcome (strangles) his adversary. He then leaves the special world he's visited and **8.)** returns, transformed, wiser, stronger and triumphant with the dead lion over his shoulder. Theseus and the Minotaur, is another one. *Star Wars* uses the same arc but different circumstances and characters. You can incorporate the items listed 1—8 to your POD book and keep your reader turning those pages!

Or you may want to trash the Hero's Journey and just wander. I think you can wander all you want but be sure to put some conflict whenever you can. Put your hero up a tree and throw rocks at him! Have him come down and throw more rocks at him!

5

The residual is a catch-all for things I may have forgotten. Do not submit a book that's going to retail for $25.00. Unless you're a published author using POD to bring one of your out-of-print titles back to life, or it's an art book or a non-fiction expose, keep the price down by keeping the length down. Revise your book to fit into accepted genre word count or page range. A 65,000 to 75,000 word mystery is going to retail for under $15.00. People can handle that much better and you can promote and sell your book more easily.

Don't be surprised or put off by the expenses associated with promoting your book. Keep your day job. Spend your money wisely and do as much legwork as you can for yourself. Just like any business keep good records. Save all receipts. Keep a mileage log. It all helps at tax time. Additionally, be open to assistance and open to success in any form it may take. I can tell you that I have discussed and corresponded about POD with more than one mainstream, best-selling author. My novel has made its way around the world to places I'd never dreamed it would reach. I have spoken to groups that would not give me the time of day but for my independent writing and publishing efforts.

Well, that's it. The POD publisher's website is open for business 24/7! I plan to be proofing the book block and cover on-line in about a week. The book should go live about two weeks after that and be available for purchase.

What are *you* waiting for? POD has new but it's changed the game and it's here to stay. You can make money at it. Can you get rich overnight. Afraid not. Yes, I still need a day job but I enjoy independent publishing and with the right attitude, trust and faith in the man upstairs you just never know. Stick with what you want to do and leave the rest to God is my mantra.

Please try to look at the process as a journey rather than a result oriented undertaking. I can tell you that my books have done as well or better than if I had a contract with a traditional publisher. Moreover, with digital technology, my books (and yours!) won't go out of print. What are you waiting for? Publish your own book now. Your dream is within reach. Do it yourself now!

One more thing before we move on to the glossary which I trust will have a lot of useful reference items. Also, I've thrown a sneak preview of the current project I'm working on back on the other side of the glossary. Please take a look at that and let me have some feedback via www.riverbooks.com. But where was I? Oh yeah. One more thing. POD prices have gone up. It might be time for someone like you or me to step in and set up your own POD publishing company. You can then write and publish your own projects for yourself and others. All you'd have to do is buy a block of ISBN's from Bowker's (www.bowker.com), hook-up with a POD technology provider and a book distributor, re-vamp your website and you'd be in business! Could that be the next step in the journey? I guess that could be the subject of another "how to" book.

Reading List:

1. The Sell-Your-Novel Toolkit: Everything You Need to Know About Queries, Synopses, Marketing & Breaking in
by Elizabeth Lyon (October 1997)
Blue Heron Pub; ISBN: 0936085401.

Comments: This book conveys the realities of the writing business with helpful insights, and invaluable case studies. Elizabeth Lyon is a writer's champion! Be sure to visit www.elizabethlyon.com. Elizabeth and her team of editors are great mentors and teachers of novel-crafting. In today's market, even previously published mainstream authors employ Elizabeth to strengthen their writing projects. She's busy but she'll make time for the grass-roots author. Also, please consider **Nonfiction Book Proposals Anybody Can Write: How to Get a Contract and Advance Before Writing Your Book**
by Elizabeth Lyon, Natasha Kern

2. Publish Your Own Novel
by Connie Shelton, Lee Ellison (Editor) (October 1996) Intrigue Press; ISBN: 0964316161.

Comments: This is one I found on an Internet search and I'm so glad I did. Although it came out before the advent of POD, it's how to approach business lessons, and common sense approach to marketing are applicable to the POD business. I've dog-eared nearly every page of my copy. Be sure to review the chapter captioned Who Comes First? What Comes Second? Beginning on page 169.

3. <u>Stein on Writing</u>
by Sol Stein (Paperback—January 2000) 320 pages (January 2000) Griffin Trade Paperback; ISBN: 0312254210.

4. Zen and the Art of Writing
by <u>Ray Bradbury</u> Reissue edition (April 1, 1992)
Bantam Books; ISBN: 0553296345.

Comments: This is great reading and will help you turn off that internal censor.

5. Bird by Bird: Some Instructions on Writing and Life by <u>Anne Lamott</u> **Paperback**—239 pages (October 1995) Anchor; ISBN: 0385480016.

Comments: A warm and heartfelt book with realistic and practical tips for life and writing.

6. <u>The Writer's Journey: Mythic Structure for Writers</u> by Christopher Vogler (Paperback—November 1998) 326 pages 2nd edition Michael Wiese Productions; ISBN: 0941188701.

Comments: A must read for those motivated to write commercially viable fiction.

7. Literary Market Place and International Literary Market Place, R.R. Bowker, A Reed Reference Publishing Co, 121 Chanlon Rd., New Providence, NJ 07974

8. Writer's Market, updated each year, Writer's Digest Books 1057 Dana Ave., Cincinnati, OH 45207

Glossary

Sample Amazon Number 1 Email:

What's in Your Food That Could Kill You?

Did I get your attention?

I thought so! The copy below was penned by my friend and Spiritual Marketing author Joe Vitale. Joe's re-working of my own promotional pitch has rejuvenated my marketing campaign and can do he can do the same for you!

Now, let's show Joe what wonders his magic words can do! Click on the link below to purchase St. Jude's Secret at Amazon. Let's send those sales to Best-Seller levels for fiction!

Then simply visit my website www.riverbooks.com and email me your proof of purchase from Amazon and I'll send you a Free e-book E-book of Joe's Number 1 Amazon Best-Seller Spiritual Marketing a 12.95 value plus a Free E-book of my latest book How to Write a Best seller While keeping Your Day Job—Do it Now! 12.95 value so a total of 25.90 in free gifts by simply ordering today. Just in time for the holidays!

What's in your food——-that could kill you?

Are you aware of what you eat and drink? You might think so, but the truth is that even "health food nuts" may not know when they are ingesting potentially damaging genetically engineered foods.

Daniel H. Jones, author of *St. Jude's Secret*, delves into sinister possibilities created by genetically engineered foods. Based on current research, his novel spins a gripping tale of death on the high seas, drug smugglers, tampered coffee beans and muggy New Orleans night life.

25

A brief introduction to this gripping tale...

Faced with the Pandora's Box of genetic engineering and set against the backdrop of New Orleans' waterfront corruption, maritime law, and rich bayou color, Bobby Grace is a sole-practitioner attorney who is disillusioned and adrift from love, life, and career.

Beseeched by a dead seaman's wife to represent her against her husband's steamship company, Bobby reluctantly agrees. His investigation reveals that a local mobster is smuggling genetically engineered and deadly coffee into the Port of New Orleans.

In order to write his book, Jones did research that turned up some surprising and disturbing facts—-

- The use of genetic engineering is now so pervasive that almost everyone consumes scientifically altered products every day. Common genetically engineered foods include soy, canola, and corn. Over 50 percent of soy and 25 percent of corn products are genetically engineered to help them resist pests and tolerate herbicides.

- Genetic engineering has produced incidents of suffering and death dating back to the tryptophan incident in the Pacific Northwest during the 1980s. In this disaster, 37 people died, 1500 were partially paralyzed and over 5000 were temporarily disabled.

- Coffee is the #1 food used to smuggle cocaine into the USA, because it makes cocaine difficult to scent by trained canine units, and therefore incoming drugs are less likely to be seized by the authorities.

- Coffee engineering is proceeding quickly, with promises on the immediate horizon for genetic "decaf" that will taste more like the real thing.

- Sixty to 70 percent of the foods on your grocery shelves contain genetically engineered components. Here's what they're saying about St. Jude's Secret:

Journal of Maritime Law & Commerce, Vol.33, No.2 April, 2002

> *"...will surely please readers who enjoy admiralty law...Jones has cooked up an imaginative and compelling story." Prof. Robert Jarvis*

murderxpressreviews

"Jones…knows New Orleans well…and his characters move with ease and…plot rings true."—Luke Croll

Houston Chronicle

"Grace lives in New Orleans and specializes in maritime law, along with various romantic and other dangerous enterprises."

Get in on this ground floor opportunity to say you read the next Grisham before he was the best-selling writing machine he is now!

Help me get there!

Thank you!

Dan Jones

http://www.riverbooks.com

Sample Press Releases:

Killer Coffee in New Orleans

Biotech Coffee Kills.

New Orleans, La. Oct. 31, 2000—
New Orleans, La. Oct. 31, 2000—Biotech Coffee Kills.
Drug smugglers using genetically engineered coffee to import cocaine. Adding a twenty-first century twist to the drug war, local authorities reported New Orleans based drug kingpin is the mastermind behind coca plant/coffee plant DNA splicing that creates killer coffee.

Is your coffee safe? For more info, order the new fast-paced thriller St.Jude's Secret at iUniverse.com.

◆   ◆   ◆

News Release   Contact: Daniel Jones (713) 463-6361

Attention: Talk Show Bookers

Danger in Genetically Engineered Food?
Author Daniel Jones Writes of Killer Coffee

Are you aware of what you eat and drink? You might think so, but the truth is that even "health food nuts" may not know when they are ingesting potentially damaging genetically engineered foods.

Talk show guest Daniel H. Jones, author of St. Jude's Secret, delves into sinister possibilities created by genetically engineered foods. Based on current research, his novel spins a gripping tale of drug smugglers, tampered coffee beans and muggy New Orleans night life.

Jones began to research this topic for the sake of his family's well being. Because the topic captured his imagination and has received little attention, he decided to dramatize the issue with a fictional thriller. His new book, St. Jude's Secret, is set in New Orleans and takes the reader on a fast-paced adventure. Rich bayou color and waterfront corruption provide the backdrop. An attorney takes on what appears to be a simple civil suit, but discovers a plot to smuggle genetically engineered and deadly coffee into the USA.

The use of genetic engineering is now so pervasive that almost everyone consumes scientifically altered products every day. Common genetically engineered foods include soy, canola, and corn. Over 50 percent of soy and 25 percent of corn products are genetically engineered to help them resist pests and tolerate herbicides.

Backgrounder:

- Genetic engineering has produced incidents of suffering and death dating back to the tryptophan incident in the Pacific Northwest during the 1980s. In this disaster, 37 people died, 1500 were partially paralyzed and over 5000 were temporarily disabled.

- Coffee is the #1 food used to smuggle cocaine into the USA, because it makes cocaine difficult to scent by trained canine units, and therefore incoming drugs are less likely to be seized by the authorities.

- Coffee engineering is proceeding quickly, with promises on the immediate horizon for genetic "decaf" that will taste more like the real thing.

- Sixty to 70 percent of the foods on your grocery shelves contain genetically engineered components.Author Daniel Jones is a fascinating talk show guest, and excellent with call-in questions. He is an attorney, originally from Houston and a former resident of Lafayette and New Orleans. For review copy of his thriller please contact: Daniel Jones (713) 463-6361.

Sample Feature stories for print or for publication at POD website:

Banned in Boston? Who says POD books can't get publicity in major markets?

St. Jude's Secret author interviewed on WCAP

Boston, MA March 26, 2001

During the interview, Jones noted and WCAP's Pat McCarthy agreed that the lack of consumer knowledge on the dangers of gentically modified foods is playing right into the hands of the same large companies that have suppressed information over the last fifty years in connection with the dangers of chemicals in the stream of commerce, namely Monsanto, Dupont, Conoco and Dow Chemical. Jones' drew parallels to chemical companies' assurances in the past that certain levels of dangerous chemicals in humans were acceptable and their current position that genetically engineered crops, likewise, pose no threat to humans. Moreover, the iUniverse debut novelist suggested listeners tune into Bill Moyers' "Trade Secrets", a PBS expose on large chemical companies cover-up of the long-term health hazards associated with exposure to chemicals prevalent in our every day life. McCarthy agrred with Jones that a similar effort to keep consumers in the dark about the hazards of genetically modified foods exists today as these same companies forge ahead at a break-neck pace into uncharted scientific territory.

Jones' novel spins a web of intrigue as drug smugglers gentically modify coffee beans to further their cocaine smuggling efforts in New Orleans. Pat McCarthy of WCAP found the setting, plot and characters fascinating.

Killer Coffee Author on WKHM
St. Jude's Secret author on radio in Jackson, MI

Dan Jones discusses his fast-paced legal thriller set against the backdrop of New Orleans' waterfront corruption, maritime law and rich bayou color. Jones also discusses the positive response to his debut novel, the writing process and the exciting entrepreneurial atmosphere of publishing with Writer's Showcase at www.iUniverse.com.

Kudos for Killer Coffee Author

Editor/Teacher salutes St. Jude's Secret Author

Houston, TX January 22, 2001

Thousands of writers who have read Elizabeth Lyon's books, or who have attended her workshops at conferences, clubs, and classes, have had their writing careers boosted. Everyone who has met Elizabeth knows how fervently she believes in the Golden Rule of writing, "Always support the writer." "I've grown tremendously as a writer and for that matter as a person with the support of Elizabeth and her staff," said Daniel H. Jones, author of St. Jude's Secret published by Writer's Showcase in October 2000. "Revision isn't easy," added Jones, "But with Elizabeth Lyon, you know you're dealing with a person of great honesty, integrity, who has a genuine commitment to and passion for writers and a keen sense of what works and what doesn't." Mentor to 30 writers in the three critique groups that meet at her house on a weekly basis, Elizabeth has become coach and guide as much as editor and teacher. With 20 years experience with writing groups, critique systems, and group process, she believes that all critique should provide specific, positive feedback first, and then and only then, constructive criticism.

"Like a lot of first-novel authors, I was daunted by the challenges Elizabeth set for me," Jones offered. "But then a light went on and I'd find myself saying, "Oh yeah…I think I get it, now", he grinned then continued with a knowing glint in his dark eyes. "It was Elizabeth and her staff's positive support, along with her commitment to hard work and passion for my novel that saw me successfully through my writer's journey with St. Jude's Secret."

St. Jude's Secret gets 5 Star Review

Amazon reviewers rate New Orleans mystery a must read

Avg. Customer Rating: *****

1 of 1 people found the following review helpful:

A vivid New Orleans mystery…, November 27, 2000
Reviewer: mia9697 (see more about me) from Annandale, VA
If you're looking for a fast-paced mystery in a great location, this book is for you. The novel opens with a mysterious death on the seas, and the action doesn't stop until the very end. Bobby, a somewhat weary attorney, takes the case knowing that the defendants, a New Orleans mob family, are powerful and dangerous. To add to the chaos, Bobby's live-in girlfriend, Magda, is pregnant, but Bobby won't accept the possibility of fatherhood. In the course of the novel, Bobby finds himself in the middle of a crime ring led by the family that likely killed his father and now is looking for him. St. Jude's Secret is a wonderful first book, and I look forward to reading more of Daniel's work. I also recommend the Dave Robicheaux novels by James Lee Burke.

Was this review helpful to you?

1 of 1 people found the following review helpful:

St. Jude's Secret, November 21, 2000
Reviewer: elizawebb (see more about me) from OH United States
This is a fast-paced mystery novel with very very few cuss words in it! It is a cleanly written novel with strong characters. And it is a quick read as well. If you are looking for a mystery novel written in New Orleans, then you must give this book a read. Once you start, you won't be able to put it down, so be sure that you have a couple of hours slotted away just to read this book. Both men and women

would like this book ~~ the female characters are strong-willed women and yet still retain their femininity as well. It's a great stocking stuffer for the mystery-lover in you.

Was this review helpful to you?

2 of 2 people found the following review helpful:

No coffee for me, thanks!, November 20, 2000
Reviewer: lpetrini_2000 (see more about me) from Boston, MA
This was a good first book, one worth checking out! Normally I don't read a lot of mysteries so this was a refreshing change of pace.

Bobby is the main character and takes on a case where a seaman dies of mysterious causes and the local mobster may be involved. As the book goes on, you find out more about the possible cause of death, an unlikely cause: drinking coffee that is coming from Costa Rica. I don't drink coffee but thought after reading this book, I would be leery to! Many other characters were memorable: Magda, Bobby's girlfriend and the mobster son and father and the daughter as well!

If you want a fun and fast paced story, this would definitely be a great pick!!

Was this review helpful to you?

St. Jude Jazzes Utah

Biotech Coffee Mystery author interviewed on KZYN

Moab, Utah—November 30, 2000

Daniel H. Jones, author of the mystery, St. Jude's Secret interviewed by host Deston Rogers on Moab, Utah radio station KZYN. In an entertaining segment from 9:15AM to 9:30AM, The Writer's Showcase author discussed a variety of topics including how he got the idea for his fast-paced legal thriller set in New Orleans, genetically modified coffee and other GM foods, and his affinity for and understanding of his novel's setting, the city of New Orleans.

"St. Jude's Secret" Creates a Stir

Biotech coffee author draws a crowd

Houston Chronicle November 17, 2000

Daniel H. Jones has a new book out, St. Jude's Secret, a thriller set on New Orleans' waterfront. A native Houstonian, Daniel is certified to practice law in Louisiana. He has lived in New Orleans and worked in the legal/maritime community there. Currently he lives with his wife and children in Houston. He did a book-signing last Friday at River Oaks Book Store, which is owned and run by his mom, Jeanne Jard, and his brother, Mike Jones.

11/30/2000 9:0

Killer Coffee author captures real New Orleans

Jeanne Jard reviews St. Jude's Secret for Ed's Internet Book Review

Jeanne Jard February 19,2001 HOUSTON

If you're looking for a fast-paced mystery in a great location, this book is for you. The novel opens with a mysterious death on the seas, and the action doesn't stop until the very end. Faced with the Pandora's Box of genetic engineering and set against the backdrop of New Orleans' waterfront corruption, maritime law, and rich bayou color, Bobby Grace is a sole-practitioner attorney who is disillusioned and adrift from love, life, and career. Beseeched by a dead seaman's wife to represent her against her husband's steamship company, Bobby reluctantly agrees. He learns that a local mob family is smuggling genetically engineered and deadly coffee into the Port of New Orleans. The mastermind behind the smuggling operation is a notorious Don, nicknamed The Vat due to his penchant for disposing of adversaries in a vat of lye. Bobby now has more than his client's interests at stake. In a deathbed promise to his grandfather years before, he promised to settle the family score someday, somehow, against The Vat, his father's killer. To add to the chaos, Bobby's live-in girlfriend, a knock-out Latina and former stripper at The Vat's strip-joint, is pregnant, but Bobby won't accept the possibility of fatherhood. In the course of the novel, Bobby finds himself in the middle of a crime ring led by the family that likely killed his father and now is looking for him. By the end of the story, not only has he exacted revenge against The Vat, thwarted the deadly smuggling scheme, and collected on the death case for his client, but Bobby has also learned to commit to love, renewed his faith in God and to life itself.

While the plot is quite fascinating and believable, it's the setting and characters that made me enjoy this distinctively southern novel so much. One can tell Jones is steeped in the exotic setting and culture of New Orleans. I closed my eyes and I was there in tropical New Orleans with Bobby Grace and Magda Mar, The Vat and the scary henchman Mad Dog, the brainy biotech wunderkind Jewel Cashio, the street musicians called the Horsefeathers and Ishmael Lopez, Bobby's sidekick private-eye with a penchant for painted-girlie neckties. I could smell the French Quarter's pungent aroma, accurately described by Jones in phrases such as "deep-fired beignet and roasting coffee mixed with the great river's creosote-commerce odor" and hear the clatter of mule-drawn buggies through the narrow streets and boys tap dancing on the sidewalks to the sound of brass bands and other street musicians as Jones colorful and memorable characters struggle against one another beneath the levee.

Although the plot is right up there with others in this genre such as John Grisham and James Lee Burke, Jones sets himself apart with a deep sensitivity and understanding of human nature and emotions as evidenced by his willing-ness to tackle some major issues in this novel, most notably abortion, religious faith and spiritual commitment to one another and God, without being preachy.

Despite some clerical errors that are common to POD books, I couldn't put Jones' first novel down. St. Jude's Secret is a wonderful first book, one I've hap-pily hand-sold to my customers in Houston. I look forward to reading more of Jones' work.

Family affair stirs up novel success for Memorial graduate

Jeanne Jard of River Oaks Bookstore and her son, Daniel Jones, a 1980 Memo-rial High School graduate, are enjoying the success of Jones' first published novel, "St. Jude's Secret." Due to strong sales, the mystery, which adds a 21st century twist to the drug war, will be featured in its publisher's on-line bookstore July 5th-12th at www.iUniverse.com.

"Daniel's book has done remarkably well for a print-on-demand title," noted Jard who has a long history of supporting first-time novelists including several local authors who have published first works utilizing POD technology. POD books are not printed until ordered. "I'm thrilled with his success. He's outsold many best-selling authors in my store. St. Jude is a favorite here because it's an entertaining, quality read," Jard added, downplaying any notions of nepotism. "I couldn't sell it to my customers, otherwise."

"Mom's been my toughest critic," echoed Daniel Jones, a Louisiana licensed attorney who drew upon his own experience working in New Orleans' maritime and legal communities to create a fast-paced thriller about drug smugglers who use genetically modified coffee to import cocaine, set against the backdrop of the New Orleans waterfront. "My goal for years has been to write a novel she'd think was good enough to offer her customers, and I'm pleased that it's worked out with St. Jude's Secret. The book's success is due to Mom and the wonderful support of her clientele. Any local bookseller worth his or her salt will tell you she knows books, writing, what people will read and perhaps, more importantly, what they need to read."

"She has a gift, which she shares with everyone who comes in, and with Dan on his debut novel," confirmed Michael Jones, Jeanne's oldest son who runs the store's day-to-day operations and maintains a unique salon-like setting in which Jeanne thrives. "Come by any Wednesday through Saturday when Mom's in and you'll see what I mean."

St. Jude's Secret is available for $12.95 at River Oaks Bookstore 3270 Westheimer 713-520-0061.

For your convenience, below is self-explanatory marketing info from the website www.iUniverse.com:

"How Do I get Started Marketing My Book?

The iUniverse.com Author Toolkit can help make marketing and promoting your book enjoyable, rewarding, and ultimately profitable. Use these guidelines to get yourself started on the road to increased visibility and sales.

Marketing starts before you even submit your manuscript. Be sure that you know your market, that is the groups of people who will buy your book, before you write as this is essential to successful promotion. Identify other books, both competing and complementary, that are successful. Use this information to your advantage. How was the competing book marketed? What about your book is different—and better? The same holds true for titles that do not compete with your book but complement it by being of interest to the same audience. One major online bookstore always prompts shoppers by providing a list of titles that others bought that are related to the book being considered. Keep this information in mind as you write. Most successful books are written for a specific audience. Trying to find a new or specific market for your book after it has been completed can be a challenge.

Make sure the title works! A good title is essential. Ask yourself if the book needs a subtitle? A subtitle is a very effective way to communicate the topic or genre of your book to consumers. Sometimes something as simple as "A Novel" or "How-to" is enough.

Create a sales handle or hook for your book. You will use this "keynote" phrase over and over again in the marketing process. The goal is to provide busy book buyers with information about your book quickly and conveniently. Create a list of "benefit statements" about your book. Ideally, a keynote should be a one- or two-sentence affirmation of the benefits of your book. Why is this book different? Why is it better? Why would anyone want to buy your book over another? A brief description of your book is not enough. You must talk about what your book can do for others. Is its purpose to entertain? Is it inspirational? Is it instructional? How will others gain from this book? Mention for whom this book is written. Here are some examples: "The essential desktop companion for the home computer user" or "The only vegetable cookbook you will ever need." As you can see, these statements sell the book to its intended audience in one sentence.

Get endorsements and testimonials. Send your manuscript to people who are considered experts in your field or well known individuals who have an interest in your topic. Have them say lively things about your book and then use these "blurbs" to build advance notice for your book. You should do this before your book is even printed. Quotes or blurbs on the finished jacket validate the book in a customer's eyes, especially if the quote is from an expert or celebrity. Include these endorsements with your manuscript submission and continue to collect them after the book is published.

Submit your manuscript. Book marketing continues with the submission of your manuscript. Make sure your book is in the correct category (such as Reference, Travel, Self-Help, etc.). Having your book listed with the correct information in as many locations as possible can maximize your sales potential. Don't make booksellers look too hard for your title; make it pop up when any kind of search is done.

Now, write a short and snappy paragraph or two describing your book. Keep the details down, and have the description be polished and concise. Keep your hook or keynote in mind when you write. This paragraph or two will become the back of your book jacket and will be used throughout the book marketing process.

That should do it! Once your book has been submitted and is about to become a reality, take a look at the rest of our Author Toolkit for tips and ideas on success-fully marketing your book for maximum sales!"

On-line tips offered at the website of www.iUniverse.com:

Please note "How to Market Your Book Online" By Dana Schwartz. She pro-vides a great outline for marketing your book. Here's a list of websites that may be helpful. I recommend immediately checking out

www.mrfire.com Home of Internet marketing guru.

Joe's had great success in independent publishing operating from his estate out-side Austin, TX.

www.bookmarket.com If you are into book marketing, book promotion, free publicity, self-publishing, e-publishing, print-on-demand, or selling your books, you've come to the right site.—John Kremer, editor, *Book Marketing Update* newsletter.

www.mjrose.com She may be most well known independent and e-book pub-lisher.

Here's a long list but should be helpful:

Adobe
http://www.adobe.com

Franklin eBookMan
http://www.franklin.comebookman/default.asp

Franklin Electronic Publishers
http://www.franklin.comebookman/default.asp

Gemstar
http://www.eBook-Gemstar.com

Glassbook
http://www.glassbook.com

Microsoft Reader
http://www.microsoft.comreader

Microsoft
http://www.microsoft.com

Mobipocket.com
http://www.mobipocket.com

Open eBook Forum
http://www.openebook.org

Overdrive Systems
http://www.overdrive.com

Project Gutenberg
http://www.gutenberg.net

E-Book Retailers, Distributors, and Companies who Convert Content

A1Books.com
http://www.a1books.com

Amazon.com
http://www.amazon.com

Baker & Taylor
http://www.btol.com

Bookface.com
http://www.bookface.com

Books 24x7.com
http://www.books24x7.com

booksamillion.com
http://www.booksamillion.com

bookstore.com
http://www.bookstore.com

Fatbrain
http://www.fatbrain.com

iBooks.com
http://www.ibooks.com

iUniverse.com
http://www.iuniverse.com

DeHart's Publishing
http://www.dehart.com

MightyWords
http://www.mightywords.com

NetLibrary
http://www.netlibrary.com

PeanutPress.com
http://www.peanutpress.com

Textbooks.com
http://www.textbooks.com

Xlibris
http://www.Xlibris.com
Writing Resources

Bay Area Editors' Forum
http://www.editorsforum.org

Craig's List
http://www.craigslist.com

Encyclopaedia Britannica
http://www.britannica.com

Freelance Help
http://www.freelancehelp.com

Freelance Online
http://www.freelanceonline.com

Infoplease Encyclopedia and Dictionary
http://www.infoplease.comencyclopdict.html

iUniverse Online Courses
http://www.iuniverse.commarketplace/learn_online/wri_university.asp

List Foundation
http://www.listfoundation.com

Merriam-Webster
http://www.m-w.com

Microsoft's Encarta
http://www.encarta.com

The Literary Marketplace
http://www.literarymarketplace.com

Web-based Education Commission
http://www.hpcnet.orgwebcommission/.

Writer's Digest Book Club
http://www.writersdigest.com

Writers.Net
http://www.writers.net

Publishing & Marketing Resources

A and E
http://www.aande.combookclub/

About.com
http://www.about.com

Adobe
http://www.createpdf.adobe.com

Advertising.com
http://www.advertising.com

Atlantic Monthly
http://www.atlanticmonthly.com

Biography Channel
http://www.biography.com

Book Expo America
http://www.bookexpoamerica.comindustry/indlink.asp

Book Chatter
http://www.bookchatter.tierranet.com

Book Group
http://members.tripod.com~bookgroup/

Book Lovers
http://mindmills.netbooklovers/index.shtml

Bookpromotion
http://www.bookpromotion.com

Book Reporter
http://www.bookreporter.com

BookWire
http://www.bookwire.com

BookZone
http://www.bookzone.com

BookZone Pro
http://www.bookzonepro.comsources/

commonreader.com
http://www.commonreader.com

Copywriter.com
http://www.copywriter.com

CyberRead
http://www.cyberread.com

DigitalThink
http://www.digitalthink.com

Dreams Unlimited
http://www.dreams-unlimited.com

Deja.com
http://www.deja.com

eBookAd
http://www.eBookAd.com

EBook Connections
http://www.ebookconnections.combestsellers/b_home.htm

EbookNet
http://www.ebooknet.com

eGroups
http://www.egroups.com

eHandsOn
http://www.ehandson.com

Electronic Publishing Connections
http://www.epublishingconnections.com

Electronic Review of Computer Books
http://www.ercb.com

Eligibility Requirements
http://www.e-book-awards.comeligibilty/requirements.html

Foreign Rights Fair
http://www.pma-online.org

Foxcontent.com
http://www.foxcontent.com

Frankfurt Book Fair
http://www.frankfurt-book-fair.com

Independent e-Book Awards
http://www.e-book-awards.com

MultiCards
http://www.multicards.com

Net Language
http://www.net-language.comreadingclub/

New York Times
http://www.nytimes.combooks/yr/mo/day/bsp/

Oprah Winfrey
http://oprah.comobc/pastbooks/obc_pb_main.html

Publisher's Guide
http://www.amazon.compublishers/.

Publishers Marketing Association
http://www.pma-online.org

Publisher's Weekly
http://www.publishersweekly.combestsellersindex.asp

Real Read
http://www.realread.com

Replica Books
http://www.replicabooks.com

RPMDP
http://books.rpmdp.com

RealRead
http://www.realread.com

RightsWorld
http://www.rightsworld.com

RightsCenter
http://www.rightscenter.com

Reader Works
http://www.overdrive.comreaderworks/

Renaissance E Books
http://www.renebooks.com

Smart Books (Books About the Internet)
http://www.smartbooks.com

SubRights
http://www.subrights.com

TalkCity.com
http://www.talkcity.com

Texterity
http://www.texterity.comartstech/textcafe

Tile.net
http://www.tile.net

USA Today
http://www.usatoday.comlife/enter/books/leb1.htm

Women.com
http://women.comclubs/book.html

Reciprocal
http://www.reciprocal.com

Softlock
http://www.softlock.com

Verisign
http://www.verisign.com

WordPop.com
http://www.wordpop.com

XrML
http://www.xrml.org

E-Book Publishers

AtRandom
http://www.atrandom.com

Baker & Taylor
http://www.btol.com

BookPeople
http://www.bookpeople.com

Digitz.net
http://www.digitz.net

DiskUs Publishing
http://www.diskuspublishing.com

Genie
http://www.geniecompany.com

Inprise
http://www.inprise.com

Ingram
http://www.ingrambookgroup.comdefault.asp/

iPublish.com
http://www.ipublish.com

LifeWeb
http://www.ratical.orgLifeWeb

Sansip Publishing
http://www.sansip.com

Simon & Schuster
http://www.simonsays.comebooks

Stephen King: the official Web presence
http://www.stephenking.com

Time Warner
http://www.twbookmark.comebooks/index.html

Random House
http://www.randomhouse.com

E-Book and related E-mail newsletters

EBooknet
http://www.ebooknet.com

Electronic Publishing Connections by Jamie Engle
http://www.epublishingconnections.com

E-Publishing Opportunities Newsletter
http://www.myplanet.netvanburen/waterside

John Kremer's Book Marketing Update
http://www.bookmarket.com

E-Publishing Contracts and Legal Resources

Facts On File
http://www.factsonfile.com

Library of Congress Copyright Office
http://lcweb.loc.gov/copyright/

National Writers Union
http://www.nwu.org

OnWord Press
http://www.onwordpress.comresources/custompub

Pamela Samuelson
http://www.sims.berkeley.edu/~pam/papers.html

Publishing Law Center
http://www.publaw.comlegal.html/

Stanford University
http://fairuse.stanford.edu

Yale University Library
http://www.library.yale.edu/~llicense/liclinks.shtml

Personal Success Stories

M. J. Rose
http://www.mjrose.com

Say I Can, Inc.
http://www.sayican.com

Word of Mouth
http://here.at/wordofmouth

XC Publishing
http://www.xcpublishing.com

More on Internet marketing approach:

You want to gain a presence for your title on the big search engines. Do this by doing the legwork initially, (on-line reviews, announcements and releases) then it will mushroom on its own. For instance, a current search for my title reveals the following:

Your search: "St. Jude's Secret"

Categories <u>News</u>

1. **<u>ST. JUDE'S SECRET</u>** by Daniel H. Jones

    ST. JUDE'S SECRET Daniel H. Jones Writer's Showcase Press October 2001 ISBN 0595131069
    Reviewed by Luke Croll. Bobby Grace is a disillusioned attorney....
    www.geocities.com/murderxpressreviews/stjudessecret.htm - 5k - <u>Cached</u> - <u>More pages from this site</u>

2. <u>RiverBooks.com—Home of Author Daniel H. Jones</u>

    ...Jude's Secret, delves into sinister possibilities created by genetically engineered
    foods....Here's what people are saying about Daniel Jones' **St. Jude's Secret**....
    www.riverbooks.com/stjudessecret.html - 22k - <u>Cached</u> - <u>More pages from this site</u>

Additionally, get a website for your book and book business. Your ISP should offer you free space to build one. I think that's the cheapest way to get into it. Be sure you go further and submit your keywords to the search engines.

If you have the money to hire a Webmaster to set it up, maintain it and get it into the search engines do it. Expect to pay $5,000 minimum to set it up for e-commerce. Keep those receipts! You can visit me at <u>www.riverbooks.com</u>.

Independent Book Stores:

You'll need to make your own contact list for independent booksellers in your area and beyond. Search in on-line yellow pages for bookstores and save in your address book. Here's a short list. Remember, if you want your books on their shelves, be prepared with promo copies. Also, If you do a radio call-in about your book in another city, you need to get copies to a local independent in advance so you can let folks in that area know where to get your book. A few chains that have lately become more open to POD authors are included:

2 Friends Bookstore 598 Cascade Ave SW
Atlanta, GA 30310

Admiralty Book Inc 8210 Hampton Blvd
Norfolk, VA 23505

Alexander Books 2001 W Congress St
Lafayette, LA 70506

Beckham's Book Shop 228 Decatur St
New Orleans, LA 70130

Book Store The 3815 Senator J Bennett Johnston Ave
Lake Charles, LA 70601

Bookstar 414 N Peters St
New Orleans, LA 70130

Borders Books & Music 9633 Westheimer Rd # A
Houston, TX 77063

Brazos Bookstore 2421 Bissonnet St
Houston, TX 77005

Brookline Booksmith 279 Harvard St
Brookline, MA 02446

Elliott Bay Book Co 101 S Main St
Seattle, WA 98104

M C Newburn-Books 950 San Pablo Ave
Albany, CA 94706

Maple Street Book Shop 7529 Maple St
New Orleans, LA 70118

Micawber Books Inc 110 Nassau St
Princeton, NJ 08542

Murder By The Book 2342 Bissonnet St
Houston, TX 77005

Northern Lights Books & Gifts 307 Canal Park Dr
Duluth, MN 55802

Reading Corner Inc 408 Main St
Rockland, ME 04841

Spencer's Mystery Bookshop
223 Newbury St Boston, MA 02116

Garden District Book Shop
2727 Prytania St
New Orleans, LA 70130

River Oaks Bookstore 3270 Westheimer
Houston, TX 77098
Phone: 713-520-9871 Fax 713-520-9871

Blue Willow Books 14532 Memorial Dr
Houston, TX 77079 (281) 497-8675

Frequently, I receive e-mails like this one advertising bookstore info:

Bookstore Marketing Lists (See Library Lists below)

We are very pleased to announce the release of brand new lists comprising over 9,000 bookstores across America. It took our team hundreds of hours to compile these databases of over 4,000 general bookstores (including chain bookstores), 3,000 Christian bookstores, 1,750 college bookstores, and over 500 chain head-quarters, distributors and wholesalers.

These are brand new lists, thus these contacts are extremely fresh. Each listing contains the name, address, phone, and fax number (when available). While others will charge you two or three times what we charge just for one-time use mailing labels, these databases are yours to use as much as you like. You can easily generate your own mailing labels, phone and fax lists.

You can begin generating sales for your book immediately with this comprehensive list of bookstores all over America.

These lists are available in TEXT and EXCEL formats. You can receive both at no additional cost.

4,100+ General Bookstores - $199
3,000+ Christian Bookstores - $149
1,750+ College Bookstores - $ 99
175+ New Age Bookstores - $39
500+ Distributors, Chains HQ - $ 49

LIMITED TIME OFFER: Order the General and Christian lists for only $299 and receive the 500+ Distributors for FREE. Or order the General and College lists for only $249 and receive the 500+ distributors for FREE. Act now for these special offers.

OUR GUARANTEE: We will gladly refund postage (up to 34 cents per item) for any undeliverable addresses over 10% of the total list. We will also correct the undeliverable contacts and issue you an updated list.

Call 888-330-4919 (24/7) to place your order or for more information. You will be able to download your lists WITHIN MINUTES.

Library Marketing Lists

Just updated: 240+ New Public Libraries & 150+ New University Libraries

We are pleased to announce the release of affordable and effective library lists. The library market is a lucrative and effective way to sell your books. Libraries often order in bulk, require little or no discount, and always pay on time. These are more that just mailing address labels. We provide you an extensive database that includes the library name, address, phone and fax numbers. We have also included the number of volumes and the material budgets of these respective academic and public libraries. You can easily create mailing labels, phone and fax lists to market your books and products.

We only selected the libraries with the largest number of volumes and the largest budgets. The public libraries in this list are the main branches and buy for thousands of their branch libraries. You will not be wasting your time and money on libraries that are unlikely to purchase your books. These lists will save you hundreds of hours of work and hundreds of dollars. They are available in Text format and Microsoft Excel format. You can choose either or both at no additional cost.

1200 Public Libraries - $89
1000 University Libraries - $69

LIMITED TIME OFFER: BUY BOTH LISTS FOR ONLY $129

OUR GUARANTEE: We will gladly refund postage (up to 34 cents per item) for any undeliverable addresses over 5% of the total list. We will also correct the undeliverable contacts and issue you an updated list.

Call 888-330-4919 (24hrs) to place your order. You will be able to download your lists WITHIN MINUTES.

To be removed from any future mailings, please send a message with REMOVE in the subject line to MediaListRemoval@netscape.net. Requests will be processed within 48 hours at that address only. Thank you.

Your favorite stores, helpful shopping tools and great gift ideas. Experience the convenience of buying online with Shop@Netscape!
http://shopnow.netscape.com/

Get your own FREE, personal Netscape Mail account today at
http://webmail.netscape.com/

I haven't used this service but it's out there. Much information, however, can be found on the Internet by searching different cities for bookstores.

Sample Letter to Independent Bookstore:

16 Mile Rd. Press
13298 Trail Hollow
Houston, TX 77079
713-463-6361 phone 713-520-0061
713-520-9871 fax

Admiralty Book Inc
8210 Hampton Bvd.
Norfolk, VA 23505

RE: St. Jude's Secret
    By Daniel H. Jones
    Format: Paperback 12.95
    Size: 6 x 9
    Pages: 248
    ISBN: 0-595-13106-9

To whom it may concern:

The buzz about St. Jude is growing.

Duluth,MN radio station KVAL's Kerry Rod calls the subject novel "the best debut novel he's ever read".

Rockland, ME radio host Don Shields says, "St Jude's Secret has a fantastic premise and great characters".

The Houston Chronicle notes "Jones draws upon his own experience working in New Orleans' maritime community to create a fast-paced thriller about drug smugglers who use genetically engineered coffee to import cocaine, set against the backdrop of New Orleans".

Readers impressed with St. Jude's intelligent plot and memorable characters are asking one another "Is your coffee safe?"

Catch the buzz!

Please accept the enclosed (2) free copies of St. Jude's Secret for your store.

St. Jude's Secret is of course, available through normal distribution channels. However, should you choose to order from 16 Mile Rd. Press you will receive a 50% discount on all books ordered. 16 Mile rd. Press does not accept returns.

Sincerely,

16 Mile Rd. Press

Diane Jones

Additionally, below is a list of sites to search for bookstores:

Bookstores

The World Wide Web Virtual Library: Publishers—bookstores (http://archive.comlab.ox.ac.uk/publishers/bookstores.html); NewPages Guide to Independent Bookstores (http://www.newpages.com/NPGuides/bookstores.htm); Independent Mystery Booksellers Association (http://www.mysterybooksellers.com/membersh.html); Bookstore Lists on the Web (http://www.bookmarket.com/bookstores.html).

You can market your POD book to libraries as well. Address your mailing to the Fiction Acquisitions Librarian. Here are some addresses:

New York Public Library
8 E. 40th St.
New York, NY 10016

Los Angeles Public Library
361 S. Anderson St.
Los Angles, CA 90033

Chicago Public Library
1224 W. Van Buren
Chicago, IL 60607

Houston Public Library
500 McKinney Ave.
Houston, TX 77002

Dallas Public Library
1515 Young
Dallas, TX 75201

Atlanta–Fulton Public library
1 Margaret Mitchell Sq. NW
Atlanta, GA 30303

Phoenix Public Library
1221 N. Central Ave.
Phoenix, AZ 85004

Detroit Public library
5201 Woodward Ave.
Detroit, MI 48202

Free Library of Philadelphia
Logan Square
1901 Vine St.
Philadelphia, PA 19103
Boston Public Library PO BOX 286
Boston, MA 02117

Print Reviews (as found @ www.iUniverse.com):

Arizona Daily Sun
1751 South Thompson Street, Flagstaff, AZ 86001, ATTN: Randy Wilson, Managing Editor. EMAIL: rwilson@gw.pulitzer.net
Website address: http://www.azdailysun.com

Austin American Statesmen
P.O. Box 670, Austin, TX 78767, Attn: Anne Morris, Book Review Editor, EMAIL: amorris@statesmen.com
Website address: http://www.Austin360.com

Baltimore Sun
P.O. Box 1377, Baltimore, MD 21278, Attn: Michael Pakenham, Book Review Editor
Website address: http://www.sunspot.net

Boston Globe
135 Morrissey Blvd, P.O. Box 2378, Boston, MA 02107, Attn: Jim Concannon, Book Editor or David Mehegan, Book Review Editor
Website address: http://www.boston.com/globe/

Boston Herald
P.O. Box 2096, Boston, MA 02106, Attn: Rosemary Herbert, Book Editor
Website address: http://www,bostonherald.com/

Buffalo News
One News Plaza, P.O. Box 100, Buffalo, NY 14240 Attn: Jeff Simon, Book Editor
Website address: http://www,buffnews.com/

Chicago Sun-Times
Book Week, Chicago Lit, 401 N. Wabash, Chicago, IL 60611, Attn: Henry Kisor, Books Editor, EMAIL: hkisor@suntimes.com
Website address: http://www.suntimes.com/

Chicago Tribune
435 N. Michigan Ave., Room400, Chicago, IL 60611-4022, Attn: Elizabeth
Taylor, Book Review Editor or Carolyn Alessio, Book Review Editor
Website address: http://www.tribune.com

Christian Science Monitor
1 Norway Street, Boston, MA 02115, Attn: Ron Charles, Book Editor or Jim
Bencivenga, Book Review Editor.
Website address: http://www.csmonitor.com

Dallas Morning News
508 Young Street, Dallas, TX 75202, Attn: Cheryl Chapman, Books Editor,
EMAIL: cchapman@dallasnews.com
Website address: http://www.dallasnews.com

Denver Post
Books & Authors, 1560 Broadway, Denver, CO 80202, Attn: Tom Walker,
Books & Author Editor or Claire Martin, Children's Book Reviewer.
Website address: http://www.denverpost.com/books/books.htm

Los Angeles Times
Book Review, Times Mirror Square, Los Angeles, CA 90053, Attn: Steve Wasser-
man, Book Review Editor.
Website address: http://www.latimes.com

Minneapolis Star Tribune
425 Portland Avenue South, Minneapolis, MN 55488, Attn: chris Waddington,
Book Editor.
Website address: http://www.startribune.com

New York Daily News
450 West 33rd Street, New York, NY 10010, Attn: Sheryl Connelly,
Book Editor
Website address: http://www.nydailynews.com/

New York Observer
54 E. 64th Street, New York, NY 10021, Attn: Carolyn Pam,
Book Review Editor.
Website address: http://www.observer.com

New York Post
1211 Avenue of the Americas, New York, NY 10036, Attn: Stanley Mieses,
Book Review Editor
Website address: http://www.nypost.com/

New York Times Book Review
229 West 43rd Street, New York, NY 10036, Attn: Charles McGraith, Book
Review Editor.
Website address: http://www.nytimes.com/books

Newsday
450 West 33rd Street, New York, NY 10001, Attn: Laurie Muchnick,
Book Editor.
Website address: http://www.newsday.com

Philadelphia Inquirer
400 N. Broad Street, Philadelphia, PA 19130, Attn: Mike Schafer, Book Editor
Website address: http://inquirer.philly.com

Phoenix New Times
P.O. Box 2510, Phoenix, AZ 85002, Attn: Patti Epler, Associate Editor, EMAIL:
patti.epler@newtimes.com
Website address: http://www.phoenixnewtimes.com

Providence Journal-Bulletin
75 Fountain Street, Providence, RI 02902, Attn: Doug Riggs, Book Editor.
Website address: http://www.projo.com

San Francisco Bay Guardian
520 Hampshire Street, San Francisco, CA 94110, Attn: Miriam Wolf, Book
Review Editor
Website address: http://www.sfbayguardian.com/

San Francisco Chronicle
901 Mission Street, San Francisco, CA 94103, Attn: David Kipen, Book Review Editor.
Website address: http://www.sfgate.com/chronicle/

San Jose Mercury News
750 Ridder Park Dr., San Jose, CA 95190, Attn: Carol Muller, Book Review Editor.
Website address: http://www0.mercurycenter.com

Seattle Post Intelligencer
101 Elliot Avenue West, Seattle, WA 98119, Attn: John Marshall, Book Review Editor.
Website address: http://seattlep-i.nwsource.com/

Seattle Times
P.O. Box 70, Seattle, Wa. 98111, Attn: Doug Kim, Arts and Entertainment Editor, EMAIL: dkim@seattletimes.com
Website address: http://seattletimes.nwsource.com/

Spokesman Review
999 W. Riverside, Spokane, Wa. 99201, Attn: Dan Webster, Books Editor.
Website address: http://www.spokesman-review.com

St. Louis Post-Dispatch
900 N. Tucker Blvd., St. Louis, MO 63010, Attn: Jane Henderson, Book Review Editor.
Website address: http://www.postnet.com/

USA Today
1000 Wilson Blvd., Arlington, VA 22229, Attn: Dierdre Donahue, Book Review Editor.
Website address: http://www.usatoday.com

Wall Street Journal
200 Liberty Street, New York, NY 10281-00001, Attn: Erich Eichman, Book Editor
Website address: http://www.wsj.com

Washington Post
Book World, 1150 15th Street N.W., Washington D.C. 20071, Attn: Nina King, Editor or Jonathan Yardley, Book Critic
Website address: http://www.washingtonpost.com

Black Issues Book Review
Empire State Building, Suite 7720, 350 Fifth Avenue, New York, NY 10118, Attn: Samiya Bashir, Senior Editor, EMAIL: samiya@cmabiccw.com
Website address: http://www.bibookreview.com

Book Links
American Library Association, 50 E. Huron Street, Chicago, IL, 60611, Attn: Cynthia Turnquest, Editor, EMAIL: cturnquest@ala.org
Website address: http://www.ala.org/BookLinks

Book Magazine
4645 N. Rockwell Street, Chicago, IL, 60624, Attn: Jerome Kramer, Editor
Website address: http://www.bookmagazine.com/

BookList
American Library Association, 50 E. Huron Street, Chicago, IL, 60611, Attn: Bill Ott, Editor, EMAIL: bott@ala.org
Website address: http://www.ala.org/booklist/

Books & Culture: A Christian Book Review
Christianity Today, International, 465 Gundersen Drive, Carol Stream, IL, 60188, Attn: John Wilson, Editor, EMAIL: bceditor@booksandculture.com
Website address: http://www.christianitytoday.com/books/

Boston Book Review
30 Brattle Street, 4th Floor, Cambridge, MA 02138, Attn: Theoharis Constantine, Editor. EMAIL: Theo@bostonbookreview.com OR BBR-Info@BostonBookReview.com
Website address: http://www.bookwire.com/bbr/bbr-home.html

Choice

100 Riverview Center, Middletown, CT 06457, Attn: Irving R. Rockwood, Editor & Publisher, EMAIL: IRockwood@ala-choice.org (SEE WEBSITE FOR SUBJECT EDITORS APPROPRIATE TO YOUR BOOK CONTENT).
Website address: http://www.ala.org/acrl/choice/home.html

Design Book Review

California College of the Arts, 1111 Eighth St, San Francisco, CA 94107, Attn: William Littmann, Editor, EMAIL: wlittmann@ccac-art.edu OR dbr@ccac-art.edu (NOTE: Remember, this is a review of art and architecture ONLY).
Website address: http://colonphon.com/urbancenterbooks/designbookreview/

ForeWord

129 1/2 E. Front Street, Traverse City, MI 49684, Attn: Alex Moore, Review Editor, EMAIL: reviews@traverse.com (NOTE: this publication's focus is on independent book publishing and includes an independent bestseller list).
Website address: http://www.forewordmagazine.com

Horn Book Magazine/Publications

56 Roland Street #200, Boston, MA 02129, Attn: Roger Sutton, Editor-in-Chief EMAIL: roger@hbook.com (NOTE: For children's and Young Adult books only. See the website for subject reviewer best matched to your book content).
Website address: http://www.hbook.com/

Independent Publisher

121 E. Front Street, 3rd Floor, Traverse City, MI 49684, Attn: Valerie Vreeland, Book Review Editor, EMAIL: val@bookpublishing.com (NOTE: Online publication, no print).
Website address: http://www.independentpublisher.com

Kirkus Review

700 Broadway, New York, NY 10003, EMAIL: kirkusrev@kirjusreviews.com (NOTE: See website for genre editors appropriate to your book).
Website address: http://www.kirkusreviews.com

Library Journal
245 West 17th Street, New York, NY 10011, Attn: Francine Fialkoff, Editor, EMAIL: fialkoff@lj.cahners.com (NOTE: See website for section editor appropriate to your book content).
Website address: http://www.libraryjournal.com

Library Talk
Linworth Publishing Company, 480 E. Wilson Bridge Rd, #L, Worthington, OH 43085, Attn: Carolyn Hamilton, Editor, EMAIL: linworth@linworthpublishing.com (NOTE: Library Talk if geared towards young children's books and related subjects. This organization also publishes The Book Report, a magazine about middle school book topics).
Website address: http://www.linworth.com

Midwest Book Review
278 Orchard Drive, Oregon, WI 53575, Attn: James Cox, Editor, EMAIL: mbr@execpc.com OR mwbookrevw@aol.com
Website address: http://www.execpc.com/~mbr/bookwatch/

MultiCultural Review
6 Birch Hill Rd, Ballston Lake, NY 12019. Editor, Lyn Miller-Lachmann. Email: MCReview@aol.com. Does not review cookbooks or how-to books. Has reviewed iUniverse.com titles in the past, including "Matters of Life and Death," by Lesego Malepe and "Araceli the Refugee," by Byron Park.
Website address: http://www.mcreview.com

NAPRA ReView
109 North Beach Road, Eastsound, WA 98245, Attn: Michael Weaver, Book Review Editor, EMAIL: napraexec@rockisland.com. (NOTE: This magazine published by the Networking Alternatives for Publishers, Retailers & Artists, Inc. reaches 8,400 retailers.
Website address: http://www.napra.com

New Age Retailers
Continuity Publishing, 1300 N. State Street, #105, Bellingham, WA 98225, Attn: Ray Hemachandra, Associate Editor, EMAIL: ray@newageretailer.com.
Website address: http://www.newageretailer.com

New York Review of Books
1755 Broadway, 5th Floor, New York, NY 10019, attn: Robert B. Silvers or Barbara Eptstein, Editors, EMAIL: nyrb@nybooks.com
Website address: http://www.nybooks.com

Publisher's Weekly
245 West 17th Street, New York, NY 10011, see website for the editor best suited to your book topic. EMAIL: query@publishersweekly.com for general editorial questions. See website for editor specific email addresses.
Website address: http://www.publishersweekly.com

QBR: The Black Book Review
9 West 126th Street, 2nd Floor, New York, NY 10027, Attn: Max Rodriguez, Publisher. EMAIL:
Website address: http://www.qbr.com

Rain Taxi Review of Books
P.O. Box 3840, Minneapolis, MN 55403, Attn: Eric Lorberer, Editor. EMAIL: raintaxi@bitstream.net
Website address: http://www.raintaxi.com

Riverbank Review
University of St. Thomas, 1000 LaSalle Ave., MOH-217, Minneapolis, MN 55403, Attn: Martha Davis Beck, Editor, EMAIL: mdbeck@stthomas.edu. (NOTE: for children's and young adult books only.)
Website address: http://department.stthomas.edu/RBR/

Romantic Times
55 Bergen Street, Brooklyn, NY 11201, Attn: Tara Gelsomino, Editor, EMAIL: rtinfo@romantictimes.com
Website address: http://www.romantictimes.com

Ruminator Review
Formerly the "Hungry Mind Review." 1648 Grand Avenue, St. Paul, MN 55105, Attn: Bart Schneider, Editor, EMAIL: review@ruminator.com or bart@hungrymind.com to subscribe to list.
Website address: http://www.ruminator.com/hmr/

School Library Journal
245 West 17th Street, New York, NY 10011, attn: Trevelyn Jones, Book Review Editor, EMAIL: tjones@slj.cahners.com
Website address: http://www.slj.com

Sci Tech Book News
5739 N.E. Sumner St., Portland, OR 97218, Attn: Jane Erskine, Editor, EMAIL: booknews@booknews.com
Website address:

Science Fiction Chronicle
P.O. Box 022730, Brooklyn, NY 11202, Attn: Andrew I. Porter, Editor, EMAIL: sf_chronicle@compuserve.com
Website address: http://www.dnapublications.com/sfc/

The Bloomsbury Review
1553 Platte Street Suite 206, Denver, CO, 80202, Attn: Tom Auer, Editor-in-Chief, EMAIL: bloomsb@aol.com
Website address: http://bookforum.com/bloomsbury/
Please note: http://www.bloomsburyreview.com is currently under construction. We will add that link as soon as it has live content. In the meantime, the link listed also explores the Colorado review source.

Today's Librarian
P.O. Box 40079, Phoenix, AX 85067, Attn: Kimberly Hundley, Editor, EMAIL: khundley@vpico.com or librarian@vpico.com for general inquiry. (NOTE: The largest 10,000 public libraries in the country receive this publication which focuses on books that are not reviewed in the big trades. "As long as a work has note been reviewed elsewhere by a major publication," the submission guidelines say, "we will consider it here." A huge plus for iUniverse.com authors.)
Website address: http://www.todayslibrarian.com

Internet Resources:

I suggest you go to a search engine and search "writers' resources" and you'll come up with more than you'd ever need from quotation sources and dictionaries to editing services and literary agents. It's that easy. However, for your convenience here are some helpful sites:

Bartleby Project (http://www.bartleby.com)
A wide variety of full text resources, including Poetry anthologies, Shakespeare's poems, U.S. Presidential inaugural addresses, and Strunk's Elements of Style.

Bartlett's Quotations (http://www.bartleby.com/99)
A searchable and browsable web edition of the well-known compendium of quotations.

Dictionary.com (http://www.dictionary.com)
Dictionary.com provides a searchable online dictionary and contains links to other online dictionaries.

Dot Com Directory (http://www.dotcomdirectory.com)
A searchable database of companies and Web sites based on information supplied upon domain name registration.

Drug Information Database (http://pharminfo.com/drg_mnu.html)
A database of drug information, searchable by generic or trade name.

Encyclopedia.com (http://www.encyclopedia.com)
Contains 17,000 articles from The Concise Columbia Electronic Encyclopedia, Third Edition assembled to provide free, quick and useful information on almost any topic.

FedWorld Information Network (http://www.fedworld.gov)
Searchable U.S. government Web site. Search for government information, documents and files.

Food Lover's Glossary (http://www.foodstuff.com/cgi-bin/glossary.cfm?alpha=A)
Need to know what achar is? Ever wondered what a durian tastes like? Or how about the ingredients in gremolata?

Forensic Science Resources (http://www.tncrimlaw.com/forensic)
Bibliographic index of forensic science resources relating to criminal fact investigations of all kinds.

Grammar Lady (http://www.grammarlady.com)
The purpose of the site is to be helpful, to raise consciousness about correct language use, and to remind everyone of the ways to have fun with language.

InfoPlease.com (http://www.infoplease.com)
Got a question? No matter if it's about sports, weather, entertainment, business or science these guys have the answer.

Internet Address Finder (http://www.iaf.net)
A search engine which allows you to find a person's Internet address. Contains over 6 million addresses.

Law Enforcement Links Directory (http://www.leolinks.com)
Contains a searchable database of crime links. The database can also be browsed by categories including: investigative tools, police dogs, terrorism and university police.

Library of Congress (http://lcweb.loc.gov)
The Library's mission is to make its resources available and useful to the Congress and the American people and to sustain and preserve a universal collection of knowledge and creativity for future generations.

Literary Marketplace (http://www.literarymarketplace.com)
This is the most respected international publishing industry resource, for publishers, agents, publishing services, and more.

Map Quest (http://www.mapquest.com)
At Map Quest you can pick any location in the world, and a map of the area quickly appears on your screen. You can zoom in down to street level or zoom out and pan the terrain.

Roget's Thesaurus (http://www.thesaurus.com)
Searchable online version of Roget's Thesaurus.

R.R. Bowker (http://www.bowker.com)
Bowker is the leading provider of book and serials data for the library, bookselling, and publishing communities.

AuthorLink.com (http://www.authorlink.com)
News, information and marketing services for editors, literary agents, writers and readers.

BookBrowser.com (http://www.bookbrowser.com)
BookBrowser is a site dedicated to reading, offering fiction reading lists, book reviews, forthcoming titles, author information and much more.

BookIdea.com (http://www.bookidea.com)
A site dedicated to helping publishers and writing professionals make money and build better businesses.

BookReporter.com (http://www.bookreporter.com)
This site has book reviews, feature articles, excerpts and message boards.

BookSpot.com (http://www.bookspot.com)
This site features links to book genres and other subjects pertaining to the book marketplace.

BookWire.com (http://www.bookwire.com)
This is R.R. Bowker's site that is dedicated to the book publishing industry.

CopyEditor.com (http://www.copyeditor.com)
Learn the trade, keep up with style, usage and new word news.

Independent Publisher (http://www.independentpublisher.com)
An online magazine about indie bookselling.

Inkspot.com (http://www.inkspot.com)
This a frequently-updated comprehensive writing resource and community, offering over 2000 pages of information about the craft and business of writing.

LitLine.org (http://www.litline.org/litline.html)
A not-for-profit Web site for the independent literary community featuring small presses, journals and links.

Writers.com (http://www.writers.com)
This site offers online writing courses, tutoring and free writers groups in all genres.

WritersDigest.com (http://www.writersdigest.com)
This is the site for the magazine, which has a wide range of informational, instructional and inspirational offerings for writers.

WritersNet.com (http://www.writers.net)
Internet resource for writers, editors, publishers and agents.

WritersWrite.com (http://www.writerswrite.com)
A great site for original book-related content, databases, resources, shopping and much more.

Writers Home, The-links, interviews, tools, and advice for professional and aspiring writers, editors, and lovers of the written word.
http://www.writershome.com/

Academy of American Poets (http://www.poets.org)

African American Online Writers Guild (http://www.blackwriters.org)

American Booksellers Association (http://www.bookweb.org)

American Library Association (http://www.ala.org)

American Medical Writers Association (http://www.amwa.org)

American Society of Journalists and Authors (http://www.asja.org)

Asian American Writer's Workshop (http://www.panix.com/~aaww)

Associated Writing Programs (http://www.gmu.edu/departments/awp)

Association of Booksellers for Children (http://www.abfc.com)

Association of Health Care Journalists (http://www.ahcj.umn.edu)

Audio Publishers Association (http://www.audiopub.org)

Canadian Booksellers Association (http://www.cbabook.org)

Center for Arts and Culture (http://www.culturalpolicy.org/)

Children's Book Council (http://www.cbcbooks.org)

Christian Booksellers Association (http://www.cbaonline.org)

Christian Writers Fellowship International (http://www.cwfi-online.org)

Editorial Freelancers Association (http://www.the-efa.org)

Horror Writers Association (http://www.horror.org)

Independent Mystery Booksellers Association (http://www.mysterybooksellers.com)

International Women's Writing Guild (http://www.iwwg.com)

Modern Language Association (http://www.mla.org)

Mystery Writers of America (http://www.mysterywriters.net)

National Association of Science Writers (http://www.nasw.org)

National Book Critics Circle (http://www.publishersweekly.com/nbcc)

National Book Foundation (http://www.publishersweekly.com/nbf)

National Endowment for the Arts (http://www.arts.endow.gov)

National Education Writers Association (http://www.ewa.org)

National Writers Union (http://www.nwu.org)

PEN America Center (http://www.pen.org)

Publishers Marketing Association (http://www.pma-online.org)

Romance Writers Association of America (http://www.rwanational.com)

Science Fiction and Fantasy Writers of America (http://www.sfwa.org)

Small Publishers Association of North America (http://www.spannet.org)

Society of Technical Communicators (http://www.stc.org)

Society of American Business Editors and Writers (http://www.sabew.org)

Western Writers of America (http://www.westernwriters.org)

Writers Guild of America (http://www.wga.org)

The www.iUniverse.com website is user friendly and provides just about all information, links, tips, and services the grass-roots writer needs on the journey to publication. Probably the best place to start at www.iUniverse.com is with the Top Ten Things You Should Know…. This is direct from the website so you get on-line and see for yourself, however, I've cut and paste for your easy reference:

Top 10 Things You Should Have Before You Submit Your Manuscript To iUniverse.com

10. The desire to be a published author.

You have a voice. You've written something to share with others. And you want to be published. You've made the first step; iUniverse.com may offer what you need to become a published author. Read on…

9. An understanding of the iUniverse.com publishing agreement.

The iUniverse.com publishing agreement is a very important document. It advises you-in writing-of our commitment to you, the author. It details when we send out royalty statements, your royalty percentage, and defines the author discounts we offer. The answers to many of your questions can be found in your publishing agreement. As with any legal document, read it thoroughly and make sure you understand it.

8. Time to dedicate to the Publishing Process

Just as you've committed to love, honor and cherish your book, you must be willing to commit to the publishing process. You have devoted a lot of time to create your masterwork. You must allow time for each of the steps in the publishing process.

You'll need time to:

Carefully complete our submission process. Be sure to double-check everything to make sure that no details are overlooked (including spelling and punctuation).

Proof your book after we design it. We allow our authors 14 days to proof their book for any minor typos and corrections. Be thorough. We only provide this opportunity to authors one time.

Work with your Publishing Services Associate, but be patient. Special formatting needs, detailed corrections, and innumerable other factors can impact your timeline.

7. A Concept for Your Book Cover. We offer three options: You design it, you suggest it, or you leave the cover design in our capable hands.

We know that you have spent a lot of time working on your manuscript. Your book jacket deserves the same time and attention. We've all heard "You can't judge a book by its cover." In the book world that statement is simply not true. The cover of a book is the first thing your reader - and potential booksellers - will see. With so much competition in the marketplace, your book needs to stand out. We suggest you look at other books in the same genre as yours for ideas.

We offer three options for jacket design:

Have your book cover professionally designed. Check our job board, or contact a local college or art school. Literary Marketplace also lists designers and artists.

Provide us with suggestions and images that illustrate your design concept. Be detailed, but realize that the design we deliver will be our interpretation of your idea. If you want your idea reproduced exactly, we suggest you choose Option 1. And make sure you own the rights to any art you submit. Copyright infringement is a no-no.

Let our designers create your jacket. If you don't want to provide a finished cover or electronic images or even if you don't want to make suggestions, we can create a cover for you. Remember, we won't read your book; our designers will create a cover based on the title, category and marketing description you provide at submission.

6. Learn about the benefits (and limitations) of Print-On-Demand

Print-On-Demand (POD) technology is still relatively new. While iUniverse.com opens the publishing door to authors, not all booksellers have embraced the concept. Unlike traditional publishing where thousands of books are printed at a time and then warehoused, awaiting sales, Print-On-Demand prints a book only when an order is placed. Some booksellers may not fully understand the concept of this 'virtual inventory'. We have found that once booksellers are educated about the benefits of Print-On-Demand, they are more willing to order books. We rely on our authors to work with iUniverse.com to help us educate the bookselling industry.

The traditional publishing model prints books thousands of copies at a time, making the cost to print a small percentage of a book's selling price. POD only produces books to fulfill orders as they are placed. While this is a much more efficient method with advantages to author's and reseller's alike, the cost to print currently represents a much higher percentage of the selling price of POD titles. That said, we do our best to price our books competitively with similar books in the market.

5. A Willingness to Market and Promote Your Book

iUniverse.com partners with our author for success. We assign an ISBN, manufacture the book, list it in Books-In-Print and the databases of major book wholesalers, and make sure it's listed with major 'dot com' booksellers like

Amazon.com and Barnes & Noble.com. We don't offer any title or author-specific marketing or sales services; we rely on our authors to do that. And there is never a guarantee of in-store shelving or author appearances at any bookstore or retailer.

We do offer information and tools to help our authors prepare and carry out their marketing plans. Be sure to visit our Author Toolkit.

It's the place to go for the information and advice you need to take your book from an idea to bookstore shelves across the nation. Whether you need help finding an agent, editing your manuscript, or marketing and selling the final product, our Author Toolkit is packed with hints, tips, and how-to's, plus feature articles from pros who know how to succeed. And best of all, its free!

4. A Manuscript Ready for Publication (Remember the world will see it just as you send it to us!)

We created our publishing programs to meet the need of the author who is ready to publish NOW or one who wants total control over their publishing destiny.

—We rely on our authors to submit a fully edited, complete, market-ready manuscript. We are able to keep our publishing fees low as we do not offer any proofreading or editing services. We provide the opportunity for authors to review an online proof to catch up to 25 minor errors. If you find that you need to make more changes or feel that your manuscript needs more editing or proofreading, you can always stop the publishing process and resubmit your revised, improved manuscript later.

While iUniverse.com has opened the door to publishing, we may not be for everyone. In order to publish the large number of manuscripts that we get, we have streamlined our processes to be as simple and timely as possible. Some manuscripts or types of books may require services that iUniverse.com can't provide. We want to be realistic and know you will appreciate that.

3. A working knowledge of computers

iUniverse.com is an internet company. Our relationship with our authors is based on the assumption that they know and understand computer basics and have a working knowledge of the Internet. We will use terms like "download," "URL", and "link" in our instructions and count on our authors to have an understanding of these basics.

Our publishing process also requires that you have certain software on your computer. These include word processing software like Microsoft Word, WordPerfect, or Claris Works. You'll also need <u>Adobe Acrobat Reader</u> so that you can access PDF files of your manuscript and cover during the proofing process. You can download it now, but we'll remind you later too. We realize there may be authors who wish to publish with us but may not be as familiar with all of the latest technology. If you are in this group and still wish to publish with iUniverse.com, we suggest you enlist the help of relative, friend, or neighbor.

2. A valid email account

iUniverse.com is an online company and we rely on email to communicate with our authors. To work with iUniverse.com you'll need a valid email address.

Don't have an email account? Getting one is as simple as clicking your mouse. Your Internet Service Provider (ISP) may offer email addresses. Why not create one just for your book? Your ISP may offer free web page hosting too. You can create an 'eBusiness' of your own just to sell and market your book. Imagine having a Website and email address just for your book.

Many Internet companies offer free email accounts to users. For example, both <u>Hotmail</u> and <u>Yahoo</u> allow you to create free email accounts. Please note, it is essential that your email account be able to send and receive email attachments.

1. Internet Access

If you're here now, you've got Internet access. You may not have a computer at home, but there are other options; friends or family who have computers and online access. Or you may be at a public library or cyber café. It's not important how you got online; you want to be published! Let's go…

Next, you'll want to look at the frequently asked questions and answers at <u>www.iUniverse.com</u>.

What does "exclusive license" mean?

In this context, "exclusive license" means that iUniverse.com is the only publisher who can sell your book in print form in the English language during the term of the agreement (3 years).

See the Publishing Agreement for more details.

Return to Top.

How are royalty payments made?

Royalty checks are issued quarterly (4x/yr) when royalties earned equal twenty-five (25) dollars or more.

Quarterly payments are sent within 60 days of the end of each calendar quarter. Our quarters are January 1 to March 31, April 1 to June 30, July 1 to September 30, and October 1 to December 31.

Royalty statements are sent to authors regardless of the amount of royalty earned.

Return to Top.

I use a pen name, do I use that or my real name as copyright holder?

You can use either your pen name or your real name as copyright holder.

However, copyright protection varies depending on whether or not you formally register your copyright, and whether or not your real name is associated with the work in the copyright registration.
The Copyright Office at the Library of Congress Website has a wealth of information:
- www.loc.gov
- Go to "Copyright Office"
- Go to "Frequently Asked Questions about Copyright."

Return to Top.

Are Authors responsible for paying taxes on royalties?

All royalty payments are made payble to the author. As the author, you are responsible for paying taxes on any royalties earned.

<u>Return to Top.</u>

What won't iUniverse.com publish?

iUniverse.com will not publish books that violate or infringe upon any personal or proprietary rights, including without limitation: copyrights, trademark rights, trade secret rights, contract rights, privacy rights, or publicity rights of any other persons. In addition, we will not publish work that is defamatory or porno-graphic or obscene to a degree that it would not be carried by a traditional trade bookstore. In addition, iUniverse will not publish books that in any other way, be illegal or include any recipes, formulae, instructions, or recommendations that may be injurious to any reader, user, or third person.

I have questions regarding the Publishing Agreement, who should I contact?

iUniverse.com's Publishing Agreement is a legally binding document. If you have questions, or are unclear about the terms used, consult an attorney.

Will I be able to write promotional articles using excerpts from my book?

Of course! What better way to get people excited about your book? We also have many other great ideas to get your book noticed. If you haven't already looked at our Author's Toolkit, be sure and visit it today at http://www.iuniverse.com/resources/toolkit/tk_intro.asp.

Print royalties are 20% of publisher receipts. What does this mean?

Publisher print receipts are the proceeds we receive from the sale of each copy of your book after discounts. Since a significant percentage of our books are sold through distribution, we need to provide discounts to the companies that resell and distribute our titles. Therefore, a book may be priced at $12.00, but when we sell it to a bookseller like Barnes and Noble or Amazon.com, that bookstore may require a 25% discount. This means that the actual money we take in is $9.00, of which the author would get $1.80 (20% of $9.00).

Can I cancel my publishing agreement?

Yes. As the author, you have the right to cancel the agreement with thirty days advance written notice. See the Publishing Agreement for further details.

When will the sales and royalty tracking information be reinstated?

We hope to have the improved tool on the Web site by the end of the year.

iUniverse.com understands that timely sales and royalty information is important to our authors. Although not part of our contractual obligations, it is still our goal to provide sales information on purchases direct from iUniverse.com as well as information from our various distributors.

A more timely online sales and royalty reporting mechanism requires a significant revamp to our accounting system. It also requires considerable changes in the way our distributors report sales information to us. The current reality is that we too must wait for sales numbers from distribution partners.

Unlike traditional publishers who only report sales and royalty information on an annual basis, we provide you with a quarterly royalty statement; it is still the best source of accurate information. We'll keep you posted.

When will the sales and royalty tracking information be reinstated?

We hope to have the improved tool on the Web site by the end of the year.

iUniverse.com understands that timely sales and royalty information is important to our authors. Although not part of our contractual obligations, it is still our goal to provide sales information on purchases direct from iUniverse.com as well as information from our various distributors.

A more timely online sales and royalty reporting mechanism requires a significant revamp to our accounting system. It also requires considerable changes in the way our distributors report sales information to us. The current reality is that we too must wait for sales numbers from distribution partners.

Unlike traditional publishers who only report sales and royalty information on an annual basis, we provide you with a quarterly royalty statement; it is still the best source of accurate information. We'll keep you posted.

How long does the exclusive license last?

The exclusive license is effective for three years after the date the publisher releases the work for publication.

Exclusive license automatically renews for one consecutive year if neither party gives written notice at least thirty days prior to the end of the current term.

See the Publishing Agreement for further details.

Are the terms of the Publishing Agreement negotiable?

All iUniverse Publishing Agreements are non-negotiable.

Why does iUniverse get to sell my book for a year if I use my author cancellation option?

We ask for a year to sell your book on a nonexclusive basis after cancellation because it allows us time to recover our investment.

What is "partial publication?"

Partial publication means that we have the right to include "all or part" of your work in a new work. For example, let's say you have published a book of poetry with iUniverse. We decide to use some of your poems in a new poetry anthology we're publishing. When we include all or part of your original work in a new book, you receive a pro-rated share of the royalties for that new book. If we used 25 pages of your poetry in a new book totaling 200 pages, you would be paid one-eighth of the royalty due (200 divided by 25).

Is proof of a notice of cancellation required?

Yes. All notices must be given in writing and sent by fax or overnight courier*
(e.g. FedEx, UPS, or DHL) to:

iUniverse, Inc., Publishing Services
5220 S. 16th St. Ste 200
Lincoln, NE 68512
Fax: 402-323-7800

See the publishing agreement for further details.
*Provides written receipt of transmission or delivery.

Can iUniverse cancel the publishing agreement?

Yes, iUniverse may stop publishing any work with 30-days advance written
notice, at which point all rights revert to the author.

iUniverse may also immediately suspend or terminate publication if we acquire
knowledge of an actual or potential liability claim relating to the work.

iUniverse pays any accrued royalty due the author within 60 days after the end of
the calendar quarter during which the agreement is terminated.

Creative Writing Samples–Do's & Don'ts
Conflict:

Here's a sample of writing without conflict. It has a definite voice but no conflict.

◆   ◆   ◆

I drew weekend duty at the office. I sat at my desk on the Leviathan Lines
Tower's thirtieth floor gazing out from my great glass work place above Poydras.
The sun set red above the big river, wisps of white smoke clung to its fiery
corona. Marsh fires and cane burned down in the river parishes. I turned from
the flat, gray river and read the telex message in my hand, vacant and unmoved.
It was addressed to me, RLG/CLAIMS at LEVISHIP/NOLA. It came from Captain Klondyke, master of the Nathan Bedford Forrest, one of Leviathan's barge
carrying ships.

There was a time when I enjoyed receiving messages from the vessels that sailed in Leviathan's fleet. The notion that a ship steaming over the seven seas bound for exotic ports of call would contact me for guidance had a romantic quality I once relished. A vicarious journey. Messages in bottles came to me, bounced off a satellite at the speed of radio waves, carrying me away to brown samba rocking Rio and white washed cities on the Aegean. Moreover, I once cared about the contents of each telex bottle I received.

Far away, a lone copy machine hummed. I went over Klondyke's dire message once more. Able-Bodied seaman Terrell Scragg did not turn to for his watch that morning as the Forrest anchored in Guam. All hands mustered and the vessel searched. No Scragg. Last seen by the crew at mess the night before. Local authorities alerted. A body found washed ashore. Unrecognizable. Naval intelligence made a positive identification through dental records. Klondyke concluded with a request for instructions as to notifying next of kin and repatriation and a promise to keep me updated.

I did not know Scragg. No prior claims came to mind. He was not a permanent crewmember. He likely signed ship's articles only recently. I did not know whether or not he had family or where he was from. All I knew was that it was over for him. He made his decisions and took his turns in life only to end up dead and unrecognizable on a beach in Guam. Crab food. Shark bait.

I didn't know Scragg but I knew Captain Klondyke. I knew and liked him. I got to know him during various shipboard investigations and visits to the Forrest while she was in port. Physically, he looked like what I thought a ship's captain should look like. He stood well over six feet tall. His body was lean yet powerful as demonstrated by his muscular forearms, thick wrists and broad shoulders. His deep set eyes emanated a warm and genuine kindness and patience that he felt for his men and for me, the claims guy who often stretched just a moment of the Captain's time into an afternoon getting away from the slow paced desk life.

Klondyke came from Yankee seafaring country. New Bedford. I'd never known anyone from that part of the country. I grew up in South Louisiana where dreams and myth seep into the soul early on and loom phantom like in the psyche on until death. Generally, I thought of North easterners as pragmatic people with little time for romance, lost causes or the lazy flow of life along the river. However, as I came to know him and witnessed his admiration and respect for his crew and the crew's reciprocal feelings for him which they demonstrated through their efficiency and superb safety record, I realized that Klondyke was as steeped in dreams and myth as the Cajuns and Creoles I knew who found mystery in their wild world where the moon hung yellow in still water. After all,

Klondyke sprang from a heritage wherein men left their loved ones to test their faith against the great and mysterious world ocean in love and hate, hope and desperation.

Now, Captain Klondyke stood over one of his men's sea rotted corpse in Guam. First with the most. That was General Nathan Bedford Forrest's strategy during our Civil War. The Captain and I were last with the least as far as Terrell Scragg was concerned. There was nothing we could do in the face of the sea's merciless claim. Nothing but clean up a bit. Get his belongings and remains home to somebody or nobody.

I opened a drawer at my synthetic wood work station. The contents were disordered, mostly pieces of mail I grabbed by the handful and shoved in the drawer to keep up a diligent and organized appearance. The items tended to be low priority or things I did not know what to do with yet. I fished out a pair of scissors from beneath the pile. I wondered if Scragg might fall in the drawer? No. Scragg belonged on my desk top. High priority material. For a while at least. Real at first then fading from the senses into unreality. Urgent? Or can it wait? That was the prioritization of paper and people.

Scragg was a dead man. That called for action. Coordinate with the Marine Department on shipping the body home and notifying next of kin. My voice trying to contact and console. Long silences_ "Is this a joke?" Screaming babies in the fuzzy long distance background. Guilt for feeling glad it wasn't me. An autopsy in Guam. Small operating theater in a Quonset hut beneath swaying palms. White lizards darting across the concrete floor. Sweat on the coroner's brow measuring and weighing the organs. Advise underwriters of the loss. Advise all concerned of the body's flight itinerary. Then, of course, there would be the unexpected. Something missing. Something that worked to make the decedent whole in life would now be focused upon in hopes of keeping him whole in death. I would search the earth for a wedding ring, a St. Christopher's medal, and the dead man's dentures.

Scragg's family would bring a claim, which they had every right to do. But then the paper, lawyer talk, doctor's narrative reports and money would run their life-consuming course. Issues of liability, damages and settlement ebbing and flowing in a correspondence river running through my desk eroding all Crag's human identity as his life became a commodity bobbing in the flotsam of euphemistic double talk, bargained for at a price Leviathan could live with and a plaintiff's lawyer could live on.

I cut into Klondike's telex, carefully trimming letters out on my desk...

♦   ♦   ♦

Okay. We can all wake up now. Coffee anyone? Believe it or not the following is a revision (maybe about the 10th) of the previous scene.

♦   ♦   ♦

Able-bodied seaman, Cilton Roy, wrapped his wiry arms around his slim upper body. His breath grew shallow and quick as the pain in his chest intensified. It felt like a sumo wrestler slowly settled down on his chest and would not get up. He snapped the silver chain from his neck, gripped its pendant then whispered a prayer to the icon.

"Most holy apostle St. Jude, faithful friend of Jesus and saint of hopeless cases. Get me through this and I promise to do you right when I get home. Rena and me, we'll make a fine altar in your honor. Amen."

A heavy foot locker slid across the linoleum floor and banged loudly into the wall. His bunkmate, Beans Goodoe, chief cook aboard the Leviathan Lines container ship Nathan Bedford Forrest sat beside him on the edge of the bed, his thumb on Cilton's cold wrist.

"Amen!" Beans exclaimed. "We in for a wild ride tonight. They don't pay us enough for this white-knuckle crap."

"Last thing I need if I'm gonna' make New Orleans," Cilton gazed at the small picture frame that contained a family portrait photograph of him with his wife, Rena, and their son, Torrance.

"Shape I'm in now, I can't handle any wait. I made Limon and Port Everglades, but the pain weren't so bad."

Cilton bit his lip as he watched Beans' usually calm and jovial eyes dart nervously from the flickering light bulb above the sink to his black wristwatch.

"A hundred and eighty!" Beans shouted. "Man, your heart going like there's no tomorrow. What'd the medic say?"

"Gave me some aspirin this morning and some more this after-noon. Told me stay in bed rest of the trip. Lay off coffee and cigrettes. Just a little high blood pressure."

"Blood pressure?" Beans scoffed. "You tell him you got chest pains?"

"No," Cilton frowned. "Just told him I had a headache and some dizziness."

"Number one, your pulse galloping like a race horse. Two, you cold as ice and three, your skin gone from black to gray," Beans said anxiously as he counted on his meaty brown fingers. "You having a heart attack!"

Cilton repositioned himself on his side with his back to Beans. The pain eased slightly and for a moment, Cilton breathed more easily.

"Shut-up with that Beans!" Cilton snapped. "I ain't having noth-ing like that. Just some blood pressure trouble. Medic says I ain't the only one this trip, but ain't anybody losing time over it. The bosun get wind I'm gonna be losing time, he'll run my ass off this ship. I got two mouths to feed at home. I need this job permanent."

"You ain't gonna be nothing but permanent dead if they don't get you off this ship to a hospital!" Beans bellowed above the sound of wave wash that resonated loudly throughout the cabin.

Cilton gritted his teeth in silence. The diesel fuel oil odor which saturated the ship's air conditioning system and permeated the crew's clothing and skin irritated his nose. He sneezed and the pain in his chest became unbearable.

"Jesus!" Cilton screamed.

"I'm gone to get the medic!" Beans cried as he bounded to the cabin door. "That's it. He gonna' get you off this ship!"

"No!" Cilton pleaded.

He rolled over in his bunk and reached for Beans. It was too late. He was gone. Dim, fluorescent light leaked from the corridor through the half-open door into the lime-green cabin. The sea thundered against the hull, then died down until he could barely hear it above the single screw ship's fifty-seven-thousand horse-power diesel engine's drone. The baleful groan of the eight-hundred-foot hull's stressed steel plating reverberated as the ship pitched between rollers. Cilton grimaced while the pain gripped his heart again. His limbs tingled with numbness. He tucked his skinny legs up under his arms, curled himself into a fetal position and rested his head on his shoulder. He listened inwardly to the rapid flow of blood through his heart as it mimicked the sea's swell.

He closed his eyes tightly and thought of the secret sea sound he'd heard as a child when he held a seashell to his ear and first daydreamed of blue water and far away places. He counted to ten and then he though of Rena. He breathed deeply as the pain eased.

If only he could get to Rena, who'd gotten him to accept Jesus into his heart. He thought of her singing, praising God's name while she soothed him with hot bath suds, cleansing him and rejuvenating his soul him each time he returned from the sea.

Suddenly, someone grabbed him and pulled him to the cold floor. He opened his eyes. Two shadows loomed over him. Cilton squirmed as someone tightly gripped his wrist. He didn't have the strength to pull free, but he managed to roll from side to side.

"Give it to him," said one shadow impatiently to the other.

"Keep him still!" whispered the other angrily.

"C'mon! No loose ends," said the first shadow as he drove his knees into Cilton's chest. "Give it to him now!"

Then something stabbed into Cilton's arm. Pain followed by adrenalin surged through his body and he threw the weight off of his chest. He staggered to the sink and grabbed his young family's framed portrait. He kissed it, held it closely to his chest and collapsed.

◆   ◆   ◆

Now, I think a sample of <u>weaving</u> color, odor, taste and smells (COTS) into a scene may be helpful. First, we'll see a sample of dumping COTS then a sample of weaving.

◆   ◆   ◆

After the show I went back up to her office. I stuck my head in the door to congratulate her on her performance but she was already onto something else. She told me she had something to show me. Down at the family's camp down by Golden Meadow. She told me it had to do with the business and the cash flow at the club. I thought maybe there would be some answers down there. I went for the Checker while she changed. When the Checker huffed along curbside, she stepped out from under the victory arch. I opened her door and settled her in the big front seat. She wore a creamy blouse and turban, red lips, dark glasses and dark slacks. Magda Mar in cognito.

When you drive the mile span high above the river to the west bank, you leave a city built with human souls in mind and enter a concrete sprawl built to service automobiles. Fast food drive-in shacks, fast cash motor banks and fast fix-a-flat garages line congested roads under constant construction to keep up with ever increasing numbers of automobiles. There are a few old neighborhoods that rest easy below patient oaks where people relax in their own funkiness, but generally, the area consists of new developments designed to provide the easiest access to the various fast establishments.

As you slap on out old highway ninety the redbone road leans close in on neon motor courts, and clapboard honky tonks then stretches through fallow cane fields into cypress swamps and green scum bogs. The drive gets lonely when you dive south on the state blacktop. Yellow crud water ripples around black gator heads that peak at you amber-eyed from beneath pleistocene ferns. You think maybe you're somewhere where nature's still ahead of the game. Then you see an oil company canal cut through the marsh with salt water rot cattails spreading from the gash and a cypress shack on bricks in the shadow of a home satellite dish. You think again.

That's a big chunk of description, lots of telling, no showing. Now, take a look at a <u>revision</u>:

"I rest my case," Ishmael said proudly as he stared outside at a swaying, green cane field that gave way to a yellow scum bog and beyond that a dark cypress swamp.

"We'll see," Bobby said.

Yellow crud water rippled around black gator heads that peeked out amber-eyed from beneath Cretaceous era ferns. Bobby thought maybe nature was still ahead of the game, until he saw an oil company canal cut through the marsh, with salt water rot cat-tails spreading from the gash, and a cypress shack on piers in the shadow of a home satellite dish. He shoved a tape into the cassette player mounted under the dash. The car's rear speakers blared the murky, self-indulgent chords of the Stones' Exile on Main Street.

"Let me ask you something, chief," Ishmael said setting his smoldering stogie in the dash's ashtray. "How come every time I get in this car you got the same tape playing?"

"You need a few old reliables making your way through life Ishmael. You've got your ties and your comic books."

"I hear you, but sometimes you've got to be able to let things go. How long you been listening to this? Since High School?"

"I guess so. That's about when it came out," Bobby said tersely.

The question annoyed Bobby. Yvette, Magda, now Ishmael. Everyone seemed to have a peg on his life except him. He punched the button on the tape player to eject the tap, then turned off the radio.

"Don't get me wrong. I like the music," Ishmael said. "Something bothering you, chief?"

"It doesn't matter," Bobby shrugged.

"You and Magda still tight?"

Bobby felt a sharp twinge of pain that started in his right buttocks and shot down into his right foot. He squirmed in his seat, then took his black wallet out of his right hip-pocket and placed it on the seat beside him.

"What kind of question is that?" he demanded glancing quickly at Ishmael. "Let's stick to the matter at hand."

"No problem, Bobby."

But no matter how hard he tried to keep his own mind on track, Bobby's thoughts centered on Magda Mar, family and fatherhood as they cruised the steaming afternoon toward the intruding Gulf. The low-pitched hum of the car's tires on the road, and the sucking sound from Ishmael's half-opened window underscored Bobby's recollection of that morning's anxiety-ridden discussion with Magda.

"Where the hell were you when I found you?" Bobby screamed at Magda. "Dancing naked down at that Burgundy dive with Mad Dog Cashio and doing enough blow to keep the cartels in business forever."

"That's right. I don't deny it. But you took me away from all that. You nurtured me and gave me my life back. You made me love you and now I'm carrying your child. You think you can just toss me over if things change or start to inconvenience you."

Ishmael cleared his throat loudly, then spit out the window, ending Bobby's preoccupation.

"The Gulf's eating away everything down here," Ishmael commented as they observed tide-ravaged marshes and mud flats no longer replenished by an unfettered river.

"The levee's done its job, but there's been a price," replied Bobby.

Because of the levee, gone forever were the spring floods of fresh water and sediment.

"Looks like we're here, chief."

They slowed and turned off the road toward the river, then drove up and over the levee. They descended over oyster shells…
Daniel H. Jones 63

Moving right along. Let's look at a scene hook and then the **Ticking Clock.**

"Listen!" he stomped his feet loudly on the crushed, oyster shells.

"What you said back there," he swallowed and looked deeply in her eyes. "I guess I was too caught up in you all the time. It was just one of those things."

"My life was going too fast back then," Yvette stared back at him. "I was so young and you were a grown man making you way in the world. I used to wonder how come you let it happen, if you weren't really ready for it," she said with a worried glance.

"In many ways," Bobby ran his hand through his thick, salt-and-pepper hair. "I guess, I sort of had an extended adolescence. I haven't always used the best judgment in affairs of the heart,"

Bobby said.

"I'll second that," she frowned then stepped away from him and looked him up and down shaking her head slowly. "Lord's got a plan. Things happen way they do for a reason."

She smiled broadly, revealing straight white teeth behind her full lips. She took both his hands squeezed them tightly. Bobby again felt the urge to kiss her and he put his arms around her long waist.

"Something else you gotta' know, cher," she put her hands on his chest and pushed him back. "I told you Cilton was my cousin," she paused, sucking in the humid air before she finally spoke. "He was my brother. My half brother. We had the same mama. Different daddy. My daddy killed Cilton's father when he found out he'd been seeing mama." Her shoulders slumped and her blouse wilted in the early evening's humidity and stuck to her figure.

"Jesus Yvette! You never told me all this," Bobby said taking her hand.

"Ain't much to be proud of. My daddy did time in Angola, but you don't need to know all that," she said as narrowed her brows. "Cilton's kid is my nephew, growing up now without a daddy. Lots at stake, here. You see what I'm saying, cher."

St. Jude's Secret 22 Daniel H. Jones 21

The Ticking clock:

"I feel better, Bobby," Magda said as she walked slowly toward him and wrapped her arms around him. "Let's go home.

I'll be all right."

He glanced over at the the smiling doctor then closed his eyes and put his arms around Magda.

"We're on our way," he sighed.

Bobby wanted things to be all right. He wanted to believe Magda and most of all Dr. Marfraise, but he couldn't. He knew he had to get some better answers to the questions he asked and fast or else Magda would end up like Cilton Roy.

Daniel H. Jones 113

Just that simple! Or you can raise the stakes within the scope of your narrative, of course. Perhaps you'd like to increase the threat to more innocent people such that if your main character doesn't act, hundreds or thousands of people will suffer. Set this in motion with your Ticking Clock and you've got it!

Now, a **Sneak <u>Preview</u>** of the next in the Bobby Grace series that I hope will follow *St. Jude's Secret.* This is a definitely a work in progress so bear with me and I hope you'll enjoy this scene. It will be revised and revised again but here goes. The working title is *Flood Year* Enjoy and thanks for your support.

Big Jim Mahoney stood beside his desk. He blew smoke to the ceiling of his office located thirty stories above the corner of Poydras and Magazine Streets. It was a blue, high sky day. He focused on the quarter-mile long barge tow passing beneath the blue steel, twin bridges high above the shimmering river. Black coal in the long hopper-barges sparkled like obsidian in the sunshine. The phone rang. He picked up the receiver and listened to a gravelly voice that seemed nearby and somehow distant.

"It's done."

"You're sure?"

"Yeah."

"Check," Mahoney said. "Now, report it through claims."

Mahoney hung up the phone. He reached for the pack of Camel cigarettes on top of his desk, placed a cigarette between his thin lips and lit up. He took a long drag then blew a series of smoke rings toward the window.

"Top of the world, Ma'," he chuckled.

His air of confidence, however, belied a conscience at war with itself. He felt the hair on the back of his neck bristle. He lowered his head into the palms of his hands. He bit his lip.

"I've got a tiger by the tail," he whispered.

◆ ◆ ◆

Rabbit Ladner set down the hand-held grinder on the wood-plank deck. He sighed then shot a rope of spit over the side. Some gulls laughed and lifted off from the water as a black telephone pole drifted by on the brown river. Ladner inhaled the creosote scent of heavy river commerce as he heard the booming voice of Captain Johnny Macaluso call his name.

"Ladner, you lazy son of a bitch! Where are you?"

Ladner flinched as Macaluso's voice shattered his thoughts.

"You good for nothing bastard," the voice growled again.

Rabbit needed a smoke before facing Macaluso but he didn't want to blow the boat sky-high. He put a pinch of mentholated Skol between his lower lip and gum then stroked the stubble on his chin as he looked up at the morning blue sky. A cool front had passed through the night before with some heavy thunderstorms. The towboat's narrow forward deck was still wet. Beyond the boat's bumpers stretched a long, rust-colored tank barge. The towboat *Mister M* had angled the tow into the soft bank about half a football field away. There they had waited for the storm to pass and the winds to die down before navigating through the old river lock just up river.

"You ain't got started chipping and grinding on the wheelhouse like I told you while we're landed!"

Suddenly, Rabbit felt a weight on his shoulders and he knew that the harddriving, no-nonsense captain was on top of him. He turned and saw Macaluso looming over him.

"Here you are you sorry S.O.B.!" Macaluso snarled from behind mirrored sunglasses.

Rabbit saw his own reflection in the mirrored sunglasses that made Macaluso look like the mean overseer dude in *Cool Hand Luke*.

A face only a mama could love, Rabbit said to himself as he studied the haggard, dull-faced slacker with a single bushy brow reflected in the glasses. Rabbit wore a red bandana in his thick, unkempt hair, a faded denim shirt and jeans.

"You think this is some kind of blue-water joy ride?" Macaluso huffed as he pounded his large fist into his palm. "I wish'd I'd told personnel not to send me any of you blue-water bums! We work every day 'round here!"

Rabbit squinted up at the swarthy, man. Rabbit noted his stocky build and large tattooed forearms that seemed ideal for driving rail spikes, hauling nets or maneuvering men and materials on navigable waters.

"Don't seem able to do nothing right," Ladner mumbled as he felt the hairs on the back of his neck bristle at the sudden imposition of Macaluso's authority. "This old tug seen it's last days long ago."

"Is that right?" replied Macaluso his large ears reddening beneath black and gray streaked curly hair. "She'll see the likes of your sorry ass come and go, my friend," Macaluso glared. "Now, get on it!"

Rabbit Ladner had been resisting immovable forces such as Macaluso all his life. He wasn't sure when it started. Whether it had been his dead old man who had been eaten away by cancer after working twenty-five years in the vinyl chloride plant in Plaquemines, or grade school teachers, a junior high football coach, his high school principal—that is before he dropped out in the tenth grade—a Navy chief, numerous police officers and various employers, Rabbit threw the bit at the slightest hint of authority.

"Why don't you get one of them slopes or rag heads you bring out at night to chip and paint it," he replied clenching his fists. Rabbit felt blood rushing to his head and a throbbing in his neck as Macaluso stepped toward him and grabbed him by his shirt, lifting Rabbit off the ground and slamming his back against the wheelhouse.

"You don't know nothing about them foreigners!" Macaluso barked as he pushed against Rabbit's chest. "You hear me? Nothing!"

Rabbit inhaled the menthol-scented snuff as he realized that Macaluso was not only too big but too quick for him to face off against mano a mano.

"Take it easy, Chief!" Rabbit gasped, "I ain't saying nothing. I'm a little slow to get going this morning, Chief. I woke up with the shits and I ain't been right all morning."

Rabbit smiled up at the big man as he felt Macaluso's grip ease. Slowly, Macaluso stepped away from Rabbit and exhaled loudly.

"I'm on top of things, Chief," Rabbit replied smiling. "You just wait and see."

As Macaluso backed away from him then turned and continued toward the wheelhouse, Rabbit spat then stared at the worn deck, contemplating just how and when his bad back would start to act up. *Think you're a tough guy 'cuz your family owns the company along with Big Jim Mahoney,* Rabbit thought to himself. *Damn no good New Orleans micks and dagos are up to something with them foreign bastards. I seen things!*

"I should've signed off at payoff, in New Orleans," he muttered while he slid his hand inside his pocket and turned over a square matchbook between his index and middle fingers. "Hell. I oughta' just blow this LPG bucket sky-high."

Rabbit bent over to pick-up the grinder from the deck. He felt a twinge in his lower back that shot down the back of his thigh and into his calf.

"But I'll see you in court instead, you bastard."

◆   ◆   ◆

"Xin," she whispered her name aloud.

Her sounded strange. She sat up on the bare mattress. Through the floor, felt the incessant beat of the big drum below. She knew she had slept. The sleep weighed heavy and damp in her limbs like the sweat-soaked, thick, cotton shirt on her back.

It had been so hot for so long, but the room was cold now. A wave of sadness welled inside her. She clutched the heart-shaped locket her mother had given her. She squeezed her eyes shut before the tears could fall and remembered that while she slept, she dreamed that she was a beautiful Blue-fin tuna swimming in the shimmering sea. She felt so free. She saw her happy face on the sleek fish's body. She watched as Dolphin darted through the heavenly light above her. The eternal blue beneath her seemed an inviting and peaceful refuge should she encounter danger as she swam. But then, she felt an imminent sense of doom as the light above turned a harsh white. Adrenaline charged from her head to her tail as she felt cold steel pierce her lip.

"Xin," she said it again.

It still seemed strange to her in the way repeating a word out loud seemed strange with it just hanging out there in the dusty room's stagnant air. She wondered if the others thought it strange. She counted five other women in the room, all like her from the village of Cheng Xian in Fujian province near the city of Fuzhou. They hadn't heard her and remained asleep on worn-out mattresses on the dirty, wood-plank floor. She pushed her matted hair away from her face.

"We all have had no luck on our journey to the golden mountain of America," she whispered.

She bit her lip as she recalled how she tried to honor her family by not crying out during the attacks.

"You pay money!" The one-eyed man's high-pitched voice echoed in her mind. She'd resisted the Tawainese debt collector more than the others but he was stronger and quicker than he looked. His kicks and punches landed hard and had immobilized her during the rapes. Still, she couldn't let go of the guilt that gnawed at her insides like a trapped animal gnawing at its limb. She had dishonored her family.

The moldy smell of dust holed up in her nose and she sneezed. She felt a stabbing pain in her side. She exhaled through clenched teeth, forcing down the moan that rose inside her. She placed her hands on her face. Her cheek felt swollen and when she scratched her puffy upper lip, she felt the tingling at the corner of her eye. She stared at the dim light coming in from the rectangular, opaque glass window at the other end of the pitched-roof attic.

She put her face into her hands and cried.

"Never, again," she whispered, choking back her sobs. "He won't touch me again," she said raising her chin as she looked to the window.

Her muffled cries ceased as she heard a door shut downstairs, followed by the thud of the heavy walking cane that he often beat the women with on the stairs. She reached for the ivory comb in her back pocket. She ran her fingers over the comb's sharp points then she pushed her hair up and inserted it into the bun. She heard keys jangling and the lilting cadence of his grating voice singing left, right, left, right as he climbed. Her eyes darted from the dark door to the window on the opposite side of the boxy room. Dust particles shimmered in a ray of light that sliced through a crack in the cloudy glass. The man's singing stopped as he fumbled through his keys then inserted one into the lock with a loud clicking sound. She heard his feet shuffling on the dirty floor. The door opened slowly and she saw his black beard and the black patch across his eye. The sight of him made her stomach turn, but she sat upright and smiled at him. The bill-collector leered at her and ran his tongue over his thin lips. She swallowed hard. Closing the door with a click, she watched the spindly man move quickly toward her. He wore a black, silk robe and black slippers. He poked her in the ribs with the thick syrup-colored walking stick then reached in his pocket and produced a tiny black cell phone. He popped it open then spoke to her in the dialect of her village.

"The snakehead has your mother on the telephone," he said as he leaned on his walking stick. "Do you wish to beg your sweet little mother to come save you?"

He handed the phone toward her then pulled it back, wagging his index finger in her face. He grinned as he opened his robe and exposed himself to her.

"All mother has to do is pay $20,000 more," he snarled through yellow teeth. "She knows that. Until then you're mine."

"I'm ready for you, you devil!" Xin said to herself, smiling back at him.

"Oh yes, you have been such an eager student in Western manners," he laughed. "Little mother how your humble daughter honors your family with my Taiwanese manhood!" boasted the debt collector.

His claw-like long fingers ran through her hair. Goose flesh erupted on her neck and arms as she feared he'd find the three-pointed comb in her hair.

"Now, little mother, do you have my money? If not, I have taught your daughter so well I will have to sell her as a whore to the Americans to pay off her expenses."

The debt collector took the phone away from his lips.

"But first, listen how she honors her family now."

Xin heard a muted voice over the receiver as the debt collector held the phone to her ear. Then he pulled the phone away and slapped his free palm against her ear. He stroked the upward curve of his erection, shoved his hips forward, then slapped her again. Blood rose in her cheek. She smelled the pungent scent of oil and sweat mixed in his wiry body hair. She closed her eyes and opened her mouth.

"I'll see you bleed you bastard!" A voice Xin had never heard before screamed inside her head as she bit into the blunt warmth that battered the back of her throat.

The rusty scent of blood filled her nostrils and she heard the debt collector's screams as she reached for the comb. He howled as she jammed the comb into his groin with all the strength she had left. The phone fell to the floor. She picked it up and leaped to her feet as she ran for the attic window.

"*Muquin*! I'm free!" she screamed into the phone as she clutched her heart-shaped locket then crashed through the window's sliver of light.

◆   ◆   ◆

Did you ever have one of those days? One of those days when you're down to recycled coffee grinds, an old flames stoke your furnace then snuffs you out, your main squeeze dumps you and the ever-lurking malaise catches up with you? On top of that you've got weekend duty at the office? And one other item—a dead guy on a ship!

Why he didn't just chuck it all and become a rock star he never knew! Instead, he continued on half-heartedly with careers, relationships, and other trivial pursuits with only a modicum of success.

Bobby Grace sat at his work station on the thirtieth floor of the Dixie Far East Lines tower in New Orleans. He watched the sun rise red above the big river, wisps of white smoke clung to its fiery corona. Marsh fires and cane burned down in the river parishes. He turned from the flat, gray river and read the faxed message in his hand, vacant and unmoved. It was addressed to him, Robert L. Grace/ Claims at Dixie Far East/Nola. It came from Captain Matranga, master of the *Patrick Cleburne*, one of Dixie Far East's barge-carrying ships. Bobby noted the

Cleburne was one of the last of DFE's big vessels to still call at the Port of Orleans. PFE still had big-time coal and fuel moving contracts on the lower Mississippi and the Intercoastal but more and more business seemed to be shifting to Houston. Operations over there were growing and more than once, Bobby had heard the rumor that Big Jim planned to move all DFE's operations and support to Texas.

There was a time when Bobby enjoyed receiving messages from the vessels that sailed in Dixie Far East's fleet. The notion that a ship steaming over the seven seas bound for exotic ports of call contacted him for guidance had a romantic quality he once relished. A vicarious journey. Messages in bottles came to him, bounced off the satellite at the speed of radio waves, carrying him away to the brown flesh tones of Samba rocking Rio and the white washed cities of the Agean. Moreover, he once cared about the contents of each faxed message in a bottle that he received. But not today. Out of habit, Bobby went over Captain Matranga's message once more. It was bad news and it was close to home. Able Bodied Seaman Rashawn Johnson was reported overboard during the night as the vessel steamed up river near Algiers Point. Johnson was last reported seen in the vicinity of the Pilot's Ladder aboard the ship. Johnson had not been seen since. Captain Matranga concluded with a request for instructions as to notifying next of kin and underwriters, as well as a promise to keep Bobby updated once the vessel reached the Felicity Street wharf.

Bobby recognized the name Rashawn Johnson. No prior claims came to mind, however, Bobby recalled that Johnson was a cousin of his former claims assistant and lover, Monique Cambray. Monique had helped Johnson get a job aboard the vessel when she was still employed by Dixie Far East.

Bobby's mind drifted. The office was silent save for the hum of the fluorescent lighting overhead. He closed his eyes and remembered making love to his old flame, Monique Cambray, on a hot afternoon in a Puerto Vallarta bungalow. They'd escaped there together on a weekend getaway package. They'd been walking hand in hand through the *Rio Cuale* market area when they came across several armed policemen as they apprehended an exhausted and sweating suspect. The captive broke free and ran. The police shouted as they drew their firearms. They quickly drew a bead on the fleeing man and fired. Shot in the back, he dropped motionless at the center of a two-lane bridge over the nearly dry riverbed, where women beat their wash against flood-rounded stones. All Bobby could think at that time was to get the heck out of the area, so he ushered Monique back to the hotel *Molina de Agua* pronto! There in the stuffy bungalow,

Monique initiated a passionate love-making session heightened in intensity most peculiarly, he thought, by the nearness of the violence and death.

"Gunned-down while fleeing arrest, he thought to himself, *She could make me do anything. Not again,* he sighed, *why did I do it again?"*

He closed his eyes and saw his belongings neatly stacked on the landing outside the Royal Street apartment he shared with his girlfriend Susie Leblanc. He saw Susie dressed in a smart business suit. She said she had a job interview shortly and asked for his house keys. He gave them to her and loaded his Checker Marathon with his things for the haul to his Chartres Street dump. He watched in his rear view mirror as Susie's sheer hose calf pulled into a waiting cab.

"Those fiery eyes. That brown skin. That body. That's what did it," Bobby whispered.

He pictured Monique's pecan colored thighs wrapped around him in splendid contrast to his fair-skinned torso. He rubbed his wrinkled brow with his long fingers.

"In our house? In our bedroom, Bobby?" Susie sobbed. "How could you do it?"

Bobby knew he'd never get the relationship thing right. Susie was probably the best thing that had ever happened to him. She was committed to hearth and home but also had a successful career going. Great in the sack and she made those delicious chocolate chip cookies he loved. She was nice, smart and stable. Too nice. Too stable. Where was the fire? The passion? They never argued. Was that why he had to ruin it with her just like he'd done it with other *nice, stable* women before her? He had to hurt Susie. Or himself. He wasn't sure. As usual he did it with any woman who could throw a contemptuous and tempestuous, Ava Gardner-like glare his way. Either way, he sensed it was an old wound, scarred over, only to be reopened time after time.

The telephone at his desk squawked with its signature digitized, gargling sound. He picked up the receiver.

"Claims. Grace speaking."

"Yeah, Matranga on the *Cleburne* here." The voice sounded hoarse to Bobby and he detected a slight echo.

"I received your message on the AB," Bobby replied.

"That's right. He went over last night. No sign of him yet, but even if he didn't drown we were making 16 to 18 knots. He would have been sucked into the screws. No way he could survive that."

"Understood."

"Hold on, Grace. The mate's got a call coming in."

Bobby waited in silence. He visualized Captain Anthony Matranga. Bobby had met him at a deposition once. Matranga was a dark, swarthy New Orleans native of Sicilian descent. He sported a full beard that covered his dark, pock marked jowls. He had dark eyes and a full head of black hair. He had a fighter's nose with a deep crease at the top between two black bushy brows. His expression was always one of intensity and there were none of the crow's feet, laugh lines or other of life's wrinkles that one might expect of a middle-aged working man. Bobby recalled that Matranga was small but powerful and that his forearms bulged from years of work on the high seas. He looked out of place in that board-room where they had taken his deposition. He was good, though. He had nailed down everything fairly tightly for the company. The telephone line crackled to life.

"Grace, you'd better get somebody down here, now!" Matranga ordered.

"Will do," Bobby replied. "What's the latest?"

"The mate tells me now that the harbor police have found a body in the river."

"Okay, listen captain," Bobby said. "Hang tight and don't give any statements. I'm on my way."

He replaced the handset. He sat motionless without breathing. He could feel his heart beating rapidly inside his chest. He drummed his fingers on the desktop.

Bobby heard the elevator chime slice through the office white noise and he froze. A door opened, then shut on Bobby's thoughts with a bang. He heard someone whistling in the corridor. His heart pounded in his throat. He stood and looked down the corridor. He saw a broad-shouldered, salt-and-pepper-haired man in a tan sport coat walking away from him toward the corner office at the end of the hall. Bobby inhaled and looked down at his work station. A feeling of dread and anger welled up inside him as the telephone beckoned again. He glanced at the red light, on the multi-buttoned unit.

"Here we go," he said as he reached for the handset. "Grace, here."

"Bobby, did you get Matranga's fax on the man overboard?"

Bobby recognized the high-pitched, nasaly voice as that of his boss, Big Jim Mahoney. Bobby sensed Mahoney's usual defensiveness in the tone of his voice.

"Yes, sir," he said as he sat down and tucked the phone between his chin and shoulder. "Got it right in front of me," Bobby replied.

"Bring that and come see me, please."

"Be right in."

Bobby walked with trepidation over the thin, worn carpet as he had many times before. The trips down the hall to Mahoney's office always ended up the same. No matter what Bobby said or did on the job, Mahoney found a way to find fault with it.

"I don't need this on a Saturday morning." Bobby said to himself as he dragged himself toward the corner office.

The dark door had a fake porthole above the bosses' name. The door was slightly ajar. Bobby took a deep breath then knocked as he slowly pushed the tall door fully open. Bobby saw cigarette smoke rising above a high-backed leather chair situated behind a sturdy mahogany desk. There was a floor-to-ceiling world map on the angled wall to Bobby's left. To his right there was a scaled model of one of Dixie Far East's barge ships. Behind that was a ficus plant, and beyond that was a wall-to-wall view of the central business district and the Mississippi River. Bobby caught the glint of black coal sparkling in the morning sunlight, piled high in a long tow of hopper-barges being pushed upriver by a big push boat. Mahoney spun slowly around in his swivel chair to face Bobby. He had on his black reading glasses and frowned as he studied the sheet of paper he held in his hands. Bobby noted his ruddy complexion, pug nose and small mouth. Bobby watched as Mahoney looked at him circumspectly over his reading glasses then put a cigarette to his mouth, took a drag, and blew the smoke toward Bobby.

"Sit down, Bobby."

Bobby stepped inside the office and sat down in one of two leather chairs on his side of the big desk. He squirmed uncomfortably and looked down at Captain Matranga's faxed message that he carried in his hand. There was an uncomfortable silence that Mahoney broke with a pointed question.

"What are you doing on this thing?"

"I—I've spoken with the captain," Bobby stammered.

Looking into Mahoney's pale blue eyes, Bobby could already see the doubt and distrust there. "I'll be getting a preliminary notice to underwriters. Matranga says they found a body in the river—"

"When did you find that out?" Mahoney demanded. He jumped up from his chair and leaned over the desk toward Bobby.

"Just now. I'll get down to the vessel as soon as possible."

"Do you think that's a good idea?"

"Sure," Bobby answered. He leaned forward in his chair. "We'll need to get negative statements and help Matranga coordinate with the authorities."

Mahoney leaned back in his chair and exhaled a long smoky sigh through his nostrils. Bobby smelled the scent of sulfur in the office as he watched Mahoney disdainfully consider his presence in his office. Mahoney cleared his throat then spoke.

"I don't think it's a good idea for you to handle this."

"Bobby looked away from Mahoney. He felt blood rushing into his cheeks and he clenched his teeth, forcing down the urge to tell Big Jim Mahoney just where he could go.

"This could be serious business. I think we need to get counsel that's *currently* in good standing with the state bar involved in the matter."

Bobby watched as Mahoney ground out his cigarette in the gold plated ashtray on his desk. He felt a knot tighten in his stomach. His hands felt cool and he felt perspiration on his upper lip.

"What was it Bobby? Commingling of funds?"

"No! It was an error in accounting and the treating physician didn't get paid. It can happen with sole practitioners," Bobby said clenching his fists.

"That's right. I remember. Accounting is not your strong suit, is it? If I didn't owe your pals at Leaks, Duracher a favor-"

"You'd what?" Bobby rose from his chair.

"Watch out counselor," Mahoney glared at him. "If my memory serves me correctly, you've still got a few days suspension time to serve before the bar will consider reinstating you. Remember, you're here to get me my money back from underwriters on these damn claims, not to run around playing Perry Mason, Sam Spade or whoever! If you can't do it I'll find somebody else who can!"

The words hung heavy in the morning's stillness. The Canal Street Ferry blared her horn, muffled by distance and glass. Bobby watched as the ferry set out for Algiers. The sound of his clicking fingernails replaced the fading horn. Clicking nails. Crackling nerves. He felt his pulse quicken as adrenal signals shot up and down his spine. His neck muscles tightened as they wrestled with instinctual fight or flight impulses.

Bobby watched Mahoney as he took off his tan sport coat and hung it over the back of his chair.

"What's it going to be, Bobby?" Mahoney demanded as he came around the big desk while rolling up the sleeves on his dark green button down shirt. He stood next to Bobby. A mixture of spicy cologne and cigarette smoke tickled Bobby's nose.

"My way, or the highway, son?"

To Bobby, at six-foot-four, Big Jim Mahoney seemed about Bobby's equal in height. However, the boss carried a lot more meat on his frame than did Bobby. Bobby looked the pugnacious Irishman in the eye. There was something in

Mahoney's menacing glare that told Bobby Big Jim had been in plenty of scraps in his day and that he fought dirty.

Bobby's thoughts were at hysteria level. Not the overt, frantic hysteria, like when Vivien Leigh slapped the squealing chaos out of Butterfly McQueen in "Gone with the Wind," but rather the inner withdrawal into the psyche's screaming corners. Fred MacMurray at the end of his rope, his world collapsing in on him, yet reserved, resigned to his dictophone. Set to spill the beans to the relentless Edward G. Robinson in a good insurance man's calm, measured narrative. Bobby stared down at his white polo shirt and tan khakis. His wire-rimmed glasses slid down his nose. He pushed them back up then looked out over the big river.

"That glass isn't so thick" Bobby said to himself as he listened to Mahoney's heavy breathing. *"I'll just heave this chair right through and then—"*

Suddenly, an object streaked across his peripheral vision. Bobby focused in on a bird flying straight out from the upper stories of a neighboring office tower. It didn't look much bigger than a pigeon to Bobby. Maybe it was a pigeon. Or a hawk. But the bird appeared to Bobby to be too small and too fast to be a hawk. However, the way it purposefully kept it's altitude and cruised on a straight line across the sky told Bobby it had to be a bird of prey.

"What's it gonna be, Grace?" Mahoney huffed. "Where do we go from here?"

Bobby observed as the bird changed its direction from level flight to a steep Stuka-dive! Bobby dropped the fax message in his hand and leapt to the window.

"A falcon!" he shouted as the bird plummeted, slicing through his thoughts. "Yes!" he said raising his fist.

"Are you nuts, Grace?" shouted Mahoney.

Bobby's heart raced as he watched the blue bullet draw a bead on its prey. Oh how he wanted to fly through the glass and spread his own wings. Leave Mahoney, the dead man, Captain Matranga, Monique Chambray, and Susie Leblanc all behind! Ten stories below feathers exploded as the streak slammed into an unsuspecting pigeon, then circled over its kill as it fell to a garage roof across the street from Dixie Far East's office. Bobby fell back into Mahoney's chair. He felt as if a burden had been lifted from his shoulders and he knew the time to move on had come, as he watched the falcon tear at the pigeon with it's rapier like beak.

"Are you out of your damn mind, son?"

The words shattered Bobby's euphoria. He looked up at the red-faced boss towering over him and felt the words he'd wanted to say for so long welling up inside him.

"It's all yours Big Jim. Find yourself another whipping boy. I quit!"

Bobby bounced up out of the chair and headed for the door. As he put his hand on the door handle, he heard Mahoney call out his name in a shrill voice.

"Bobby, did I tell you about the dead guy? This guy, what's his name?"

Bobby stopped and turned to face Mahoney. His heart was pounding and he was breathing heavily. He watched as Mahoney stepped back behind his desk and grabbed his reading glasses. Mahoney's chest heaved as he studied the fax message on his desk again.

"The dead guy. Our man Rashawn Johnson. Ain't that a nigger name for you?" he smirked at Bobby.

"You're full of shit," Bobby fired back. "I'm outta' here."

"Wait. Wait. Something you need to know about our man, Rashawn, Bobby. Matranga and marine personnel have confirmed for me that you and Rashawn have something in common."

"What kind of game is this, Jim?"

Bobby exhaled and shifted his weight to his left side as he felt sciatic pain shooting from his lower back down into his right foot. From across the river, he heard the Canal Street Ferry horn blare again as she began her return to the city.

"Yes, indeed," Mahoney chuckled. "It seems that your former assistant, one Miss Monique Cambray, had something going with our man. Did you know that Bobby?"

Bobby listened but he did not reply. He felt heat burning in his cheeks and ears. He felt hot rage in the pit of his stomach, as if someone had just taken a blowtorch to his insides.

"Personnel tells me she filed on him for child support and the state garnished his wages. It seems your sweet brown sugar provided an heir for our man Rashawn."

"You're lying!"

"Personnel's got the records, Bobby," Mahoney shrugged. But there's more, Bobby." Mahoney shook his head from side to side and rubbed his dark brows. "Captain Matranga has informed me that Miss Cambray often picked our man up at the end of the voyage. He even remembers seeing her in a big old Checker Marathon. That's what you drive, isn't it Bobby?"

Bobby felt the rage inside him dissipate into queasiness. The back of his neck felt cold and sweaty. He swallowed hard and forced down the sudden urge to vomit.

"You'd been seeing that black gal too, right Bobby?"

Bobby breathed heavily as he stared at Mahoney. He wanted to leap over the big desk and grab Big Jim by the throat. He wanted to dash out the door, too. But he found that he could not move. He had to stay put. He had to stand before Mahoney, now the focal point of all his anger and resentment, and hear the full account of Monique's betrayal. He knew it was coming beyond the shadow of a doubt. He knew it was coming just as certainly as he knew he had betrayed Susie Leblanc and just as certainly as he knew his mother had betrayed him.

"Looks to me like she played you good while she was still seeing him."

Bobby watched as Mahoney came around the desk. Mahoney stood in front of Bobby. He had taken off his reading glasses and Bobby watched as Mahoney slid the extended black earpiece between his pursed lips. All Bobby could hear was Mahoney's breathing as he watched Mahoney move that earpiece slowly back and forth between his thin lips. Then Mahoney removed it and folded the glasses. He winked at Bobby and spoke.

"What is it they say, Bobby? Once you've had black, you'll never go back?" Mahoney screwed his face right up into Bobby's. "I guess you couldn't quite satisfy Miss Monique, huh Bobby?"

There it was. Bobby had waited and Mahoney had not disappointed. The fuse was lit. Bobby turned away from Mahoney. Briefly he closed his eyes and he saw a vision of solar flares, orange, red and yellow exploding from a blackened sun. Then his muscles took over and he grabbed the edge of the door with both hands. He swung the door with all his might and leaped out of Mahoney's office. The sound of the door slamming reverberated in Bobby's ears like the sound of thunder as he ran for the elevator.

He wandered the Quarter that afternoon. It started out fun. He met a nice young couple from Houston in the Old Absinthe House. Played the juke box for hours. All the while guzzling Abita Amber on tap as he gave them sight-seeing tips. The guy was an easy-going type and the wife was a blonde with a warm smile and a mischievous twinkle in her eye that made him think of a Dave Edmunds/Nick Lowe recording called "I Knew the Bride When She used to Rock-n-Roll". The couple went to dinner and left Bobby with alone with his somewhat covetous feelings. As the sun went down and Bourbon Street's carnival spirit donned it's sparkling evening gown, Bobby drifted into a he knew to be frequented by strippers, female impersonators and other Quarter service industry personnel.

Molly's Bar on Toulouse just off Bourbon had a decent juke box. It was a bit heavy with depressing headbanger fare but it had some old reliables that Bobby enjoyed. He chose Keith Richard's Main Offender CD on the high-tech juke box and stood at the smooth, oak bar. A cute Asian girl bartender he'd chatted up before smiled and set a creamy, beautiful pint of Guinness before him.

"Slow-poured. Saw you coming, man."

"Thanks, Yvette," Bobby said.

He felt warm and welcome as he looked into her round, smiling face. Her black hair cut short, almost like a boy's bright eyes and pearly-whites made her look just so fresh and appealing to him. Very simply dressed in white tee-shirt and blue jeans. He watched her cute, compact ass-in-jeans scoot down to the other end of the bar.

Then he saw himself in the wide mirror behind the bar as he raised his glass to his lips. Sturdy build in khakis and white shirt. Wire-rim glasses. Dark hair. Gray strands in a clean part. Except for that deviated septum nose, he saw a youthful face like the one the kid mother's count on to write home every week from far-away state college. The one meandering, bewildered tourists chose to ask for directions. The familiar smell and taste of his brew soothed his nerves. Sharp images of Big Jim Mahoney calling him out on the cheap carpet rounded softly into dulled, present sense impressions that oozed so familiar. The feeling of never being good enough at anything he did, never measuring up to *her* crept up and then enveloped him in a cocoon-like feeling of self-pity. He looked the other way while he sought self-destruction's comfort in the drink, the dark bar, the music and the women he knew would soon light on nearby barstools. *The Rake's Progress.* Indeed!

The juke box rhythm rolled steady. He didn't have to wait long. A covey of long-haired, long-legged girls in strip club rental cat-suits and and bare-midriff minis. One that looked young enough to be his own daughter smiled at him from the end of the bar. She was a buxom blonde, with her hair falling across her face over one eye like that portrait of Veronica Lake on Clapton's *Layla* album.

This is good, he said to himself. He felt a jolt of sciatic pain in his right thigh and as he shifted his weight from his right leg to his left. With all this activity at the end of the bar, he didn't see *her* come into the bar. It wasn't until his nose picked up a sweet scent, wild in a hot day's evening cool down. The bittersweet smell of gardenias latched onto him and turned him away from the young blonde's winsome smile.

He caught a glimpse of cinnamon calf above and followed it right on up a smooth, bare thigh to a high riding purple and black leopard print jersey dress. Her trim but shapely body looked great in the skin-tight mini, but faint crow's feet at the corners and loopy bags under her buggy, Bette Davis eyes gave him the feeling that she had either missed out on wearing such eye-candy clothing in her younger days or she was just determined to remain the show-stopping, guy-trouble magnet on the far side of thirty-five.

"What you looking at? You a cop or something!" she frowned with her hands on her hips.

He sensed mock disdain in her dark eyes. that She spoke with a Spanish accent in a smoker's hoarse voice. He noticed a turquoise-eyed silver iguana pin that shimmered above her breast. Diamonds twinkled on the first and second fingers of her right hand. A ruby ring on her that matched oval rubies separated by turquoise cylinders on her choker and matching earrings.

"No, I'm not a cop," Bobby smiled. "Just an ambulance chaser."

"You? A lawyer. Yeah, I guess so. You have those glasses."

"Robert L. Grace," he extended his hand. "Most people just call me Bobby."

"Bobby! That sounds like a kid's name. I like Robert better."

He felt the warmth of her smooth, slender hand. She was about medium height but stood tall in black, high heeled pumps. Her hair was black, parted in the middle with a slight widow's peak and fell straight to her shoulders. Through the saloon's open doors, Bobby noticed a silver Mercedes pull up to the curb, headlights on.

"Care to sit down?"

He watched her turn and look outside toward the idling Benz curbside. Then she looked Bobby up and down and sat down with a sigh. Bobby eased onto the stool next to her. He could her the racket of the car's diesel engine outside.

"I just stopped in for cigarettes," she bit her lip. "And a shot."

"What are you drinking."

"Tequila. It's been a long day."

"Yvette," Bobby called to the bartender and placed an order for two shots of Commeretivo and a pack of Virginia Slim 100's.

They shared the lime and salt ritual quickly. She glanced at him when she licked salt from her thumb. Bobby's nose twitched as gardenias and cigarette smoke mixed with zesty citrus and salt. The golden liquid went down smooth and warm with a loving after-burner and stiff kick, of course. Like any guy, he felt surely he'd soon be bonded with her at a more intimate level as soon as the tequila her loosened her spirit.

"I didn't get your name?"

"I didn't give it."

"Okay, sorry," he replied taking a step back.

"You give up too easy," she frowned at him. "I am Juanita Matherne."

Bobby nodded his head as he watched her open the green and gold pack of cigarettes. The Juanita fit. She had Hispanic features with the almond shaped-eyes, dark hair, full, pouty lips and olive skin. But there was also a touch of Asian or Native American because she didn't have any noticeable eyelid. Her dark brows arched high over the top of her somewhat haughty, slender nose.

"Pleased to meet you. Matherne's a name I've seen down the bayou. You don't look like your from down that way."

"I'm from Honduras originally. I got married to a guy from Houma."

She put a slender cigarette to her lips. Bobby reached for matchbook in a black plastic ashtray. He lit a match and held it out for her. She smiled at his as she lit up. Then Bobby heard the horn from the car outside.

"That's my business partner," she said as she seemed to blow her cares with the smoke to the ceiling. "I've got to go."

"You just got here." Bobby said feeling full of himself.

"Do you have a card?"

He sorted through his wallet and gave her one that was a bit dog-eared. She looked it over then stepped toward the open door.

"Maybe I'll see you around, Grace."

She flashed him a cover-girl smile and she waved goodbye.

He felt sad at her departure. He lost track of the off-duty strippers and got a bit sloshed on half-a-dozen more Guinness pints. He paid his tab and tipped Yvette generously as she closed out her shift. He set out for his place on Chartres but found himself drawn to Susie LeBlanc's apartment on Royal Street. He stood on the flagstone sidewalk across the street and looked up at the balcony. The lights were off. He remembered once standing outside on the street, singing to her as she stood on the second-floor balcony one evening when they first dated. She was sweet as "Tupelo Honey" to him back then. He ambled the four blocks home, humming the tune while he wrestled with the idea that he'd inevitably sacrificed Susie and any happiness they might share to the demons that danced with him for a lifetime in the shadows of his heart's fire. Shame. Lust. Guilt. Hate. All kinds of emotional powerhouses that he hooked into with friends, family and lovers who were in on the same game, trying to figure liability and measure damages just like the claims game he'd played for a year at Dixie Far East while things remained perpetually undisturbed and always came out for the best. Or did they?

He called Susie on the telephone and woke her up. He apologized again for hurting her. She told him she was over it and to get lost. He agreed that was probably best after she hung up on him.

COMING IN SPRING 2004!

Please visit <u>www.riverbooks.com</u> and leave feedback.
Thank you!

0-595-30847-3

Printed in the United States
70255LV00006BA/64